Essay Index

P9-AFK-593

DATE DUE

JUN 1 0 2004			

Demco

CRITICS ON CARIBBEAN LITERATURE

CRITICS ON CARIBBEAN LITERATURE

Readings in Literary Criticism

Edited by Edward Baugh
Department of English, University of the West Indies

St. Martin's Press   New York

Printed in Great Britain

Library of Congress Catalog Card Number 76-21943

ISBN 0-312-17605-8

First published in the United States of America in 1978

ACKNOWLEDGEMENTS

We are grateful to the following for permission to use copyright material from the works whose titles follow in brackets:

Southern Review and Kenneth Ramchand (Kenneth Ramchand's 'Claude McKay and *Banana Bottom*', *Southern Review*, vol. 4, 1970); University of the West Indies (Lloyd W. Brown's 'Dreamers and Slaves: the Ethos of Revolution in Walcott and LeRoi Jones', *Caribbean Quarterly*, vol. 17, September-December 1971); *Bim* (Edward Brathwaite's 'Jazz and the West Indian Novel', *Bim*, no. 45, July-December 1967; Gerald Moore's 'Use Men Language', *Bim*, no. 57, March 1974); Evans Brothers Ltd (John Figueroa's 'Our Complex Language Situation', *Caribbean Voices*, vol. 2, 1970); Institute of Caribbean Studies (Gordon Rohlehr's 'Islands', *Caribbean Studies* 10, no. 4, January 1971, pp. 173-202 (reprinted by permission of the Author and the Institute of Caribbean Studies; copyright 1971); Institute of Jamaica (Mervyn Morris's 'On Reading Louise Bennett, Seriously', *Jamaica Journal*, vol. 1, December 1967); Kenyon College (Karl Miller's 'V. S. Naipaul and the New Order', *Kenyon Review*, vol. 29, November 1967); George Lamming (George Lamming's *The Pleasures of Exile*, 1960); New Beacon Publications (Wilson Harris's 'Tradition and the West Indian Novel', *Tradition, the Writer and Society*, 1967); Heinemann Educational Books Ltd (R. B. Le Page's 'Dialect in West Indian Literature', *Journal of Commonwealth Literature*, no. 7, July 1969; Joyce Adler's '*Tumatumari* and the Imagination of Wilson Harris', *Journal of Commonwealth Literature*, no. 7, July 1969; George Lamming's *In the Castle of My Skin*; Ngugi Wa Thiong'o's *Homecoming*, 1972); Gordon Rohlehr (Gordon Rohlehr's 'The Folk in Caribbean Literature', *Tapia*, December 1972); Derek Walcott (Derek Walcott's 'The Muse of History', *Is Massa Day Dead?*, 1974); Institute of Jamaica and Sylvia Wynter (Sylvia Wynter's 'Reflections on West Indian Writing and Criticism', part I, *Jamaica Journal*, II, December 1968); University of Texas Press (David Ormerod's 'Theme and Image in V. S. Naipaul's *A House for Mr Biswas*', *Texas Studies in Literature and Language*, VIII, 1967).

CONTENTS

INTRODUCTION

This anthology brings together pieces of previously published criticism on the literature of the English-speaking Caribbean, otherwise referred to as West Indian literature. The fact that no other anthology of such material exists up to now, and that there is only one other anthology of criticism of West Indian literature by 'divers hands' (Louis James's *The Islands In Between,* London, 1968), is itself indicative not only of the need for more such anthologies, but also of the state of criticism of West Indian literature. As that literature becomes more and more an object of serious and systematic study, the need for critical material, and for greater accessibility of such material as exists, is being sharply felt.

The problem of accessibility is increased by the problem of audience which faces the West Indian critic of West Indian literature at the moment. Imbued, as he is likely to be, with a sense of the importance of literature in the shaping of a people, he has to choose between, on the one hand, publishing his essay in an international scholarly journal, with the kind of acclaim such publication might bring, and also with the satisfaction of knowing that what he wrote will appear as he wrote it, and, on the other hand, publishing his work in some local, more or less 'popular' West Indian journal or newspaper, where he will get the satisfaction of feeling that he is reaching the audience that matters most to him, but where at the same time he might have to suffer from the incompetence of printing and editing. And ironically, to the West Indian student who wants to seek out that essay, it might even be better preserved and easier to come by if published in the international scholarly journal, since the West Indian publication is also likely to suffer from an inadequate and haphazard distribution even within the region. The problem also affects the bibliographer, who cannot approach his task with any confidence in the traditional guidelines as to what kind of publication is likely to contain lightweight literary criticism. At least one of the most astute and influential West Indian critics seems to have made his choice and struck out a path by not seeking too actively after publication outside the region. I refer to Gordon Rohlehr, who has consistently committed most of his major pieces to the Trinidadian political newspaper *Tapia.*

Because the present anthology had to cover a whole literature, however young and small, the question of criteria by which to select and arrange the material was much more acute than it could have been for editors of other volumes, each dealing with a single author, in the 'Readings in Literary Criticism' series. In those volumes a chronological pattern, focusing on historical changes in critical approaches to the author, has been most convenient and preferred. But, partly because of the very youth of West Indian literature, and even more so of criticism of that literature—the earliest item in this anthology was first published in 1960 and all the others after 1966—the historical-chronological method did not seem suitable in this instance. We are still too close to most of the material to have a definitive historical perspective on it, and the material itself is still too limited in its time-span for enough substantial trends to be satisfactorily differentiated.

This is not to say that trends cannot be perceived even now. One could begin, say, with a sampling of the random, and usually very slight pieces of criticism from the period prior to 1950, from about which date one marks the significant beginning of the main body of West Indian literature. This could be followed by a look at the criticism, mainly English book reviews, which greeted the exhilarating outburst of prose fiction in the fifties. Then there would be the growing awareness among West Indians of the need for a body of criticism by West Indians, followed by the on-going debate among West Indian critics as to what should be the guiding principles of a West Indian criticism of the regional literature. Some other recent trends which can now be distinguished are the growth of interest in West Indian literature among black African critics, as well as an upsurge of critical interest in folk forms and influences. These are some of the historical movements, but to have planned the anthology in terms of them would have necessitated the inclusion of too much ephemeral material or material of purely historical interest.

It is because I feel that the priority right now is the need for more close, 'hard' criticism of West Indian writing, and that most people who take up an anthology of criticism of West Indian literature will be hoping to find it useful primarily as an introduction to the literature, as distinct from an introduction to the criticism (a difference of emphasis), that I have decided upon a collection which cheats a little in going outside its strict brief by being structured first with a view to introducing the literature, and only secondarily with a view to showing off the critics, their range and variety, though I hope that it will in effect have done the latter reasonably well.

What I have concentrated on, therefore, is selections of substantial and comparatively detailed critical analysis of individual works, selecting these to cover as many as possible of the more important authors. In keeping with the introductory aim of the anthology, and enhancing in some measure its unity, I have selected criticisms which arise out of and seek to promote an enthusiasm for the works under discussion. This, the main body of the book, is preceded and balanced by a section which goes in a sense to the other extreme, comprising broad theoretical statements and statements of critical standpoint, or raising broad theoretical questions of general approach to West Indian literature. (But it seemed most sensible to put Le Page's statement on language in the relevant section of critiques.) These provide a context for the detailed and specific criticisms and introduce some of the most crucial areas of theory being debated by critics of West Indian literature. I have avoided as far as possible historical-survey-type essays (whether of genre of theme or author), since, in addition to existing in some sufficiency already and being easily accessible, these, with their broad generalising outlines and necessarily fleeting look at specific works, do not fit into my design.

In the first section, 'Contexts for Criticism', the preponderance of critical attention to the novel is indicative of the general situation in criticism of West Indian literature to date. This is partly because prose fiction was the first genre to see the accumulation of a sizeable body of work of reasonable stature. It is only very recently that poetry has begun to establish itself in this way; and while there has been a fair-sized body of plays for some time, they have not been sufficiently published, and consequently there has been very little literary criticism of drama.

In the main part of the anthology I have attempted to give some shape and direction to what is necessarily a heterogeneous collection by grouping the items in three very broad and arbitrary categories of what seem to be some major preoccupations of the literature and criticism. These categories are to be taken as a mere convenience and starting point, a stimulus to discussion and further exploration. There are other categories which would no doubt have served as well—'The Search for Roots', 'The Clash of Cultures', 'New Forms and Dimensions', to suggest a few. It is also important to remember that the categories are not mutually exclusive. Many of the items could have fitted equally well into any of them. The reader will see, too, that while there is no category about form as such, some of the pieces (Brathwaite on Mais, for example) are most ostensibly about form. But form is a category which may with some impunity be taken for granted, as being subsumed by all criticism, while it seemed that there was a positive benefit, a new stimulus, to be derived from grouping certain items in terms of their less obvious or explicit concerns.

The first section of criticisms of individual works is 'From Colonialism to Independence', because the literature of the West Indies is, first, last and essentially, a colonial literature. 'Colonialism' is here used primarily in a descriptive rather than evaluative sense, although the latter cannot be completely avoided. The literature has been determined and produced by, just as it reflects or expresses or attempts to come to terms with, the colonial experience of the region. The phrase 'to independence' is to be taken to indicate not so much a realised (or even, perhaps, realisable) goal, as a kind of inexhaustible potential, a symbolic point on the graph of consciousness which the imagination can trace in the colonial experience. There is a sense, then, in which the colonialism of the literature is not something to be outgrown.

In the coming to terms with colonialism, one of the leading ideas in the literature and the criticism has been what one might call the idea of community. This idea provides the conceptual basis for the section entitled 'Relationships'. That basis may be further elucidated by reference to Lamming, who argues, in his essay 'The Negro Writer and His World' (*Caribbean Quarterly*, V (February 1958), pp. 109-15), that there are three distinct yet 'deeply related' worlds to which the writer owes a responsibility: 'the world of the private and hidden self', the world of his particular society, and 'the world of men'.

Criticism has concentrated heavily on the literature as presenting images of or for West Indian society, as depicting or analysing that social fragmentation and divisiveness which has been one legacy of colonialism, or as presenting models of community, of a 'whole' society (Brathwaite on *Brother Man*, Ramchand on *Banana Bottom*). The question of the tensions between individual and society is highlighted in such criticism, and individualism becomes an explosive topic. This kind of focus was sharpened by the appearance of Naipaul's *A House for Mr. Biswas* (1961), as was dramatised in the difference of opinion between Brathwaite and Ramchand as to what the book meant. Writing in *Bim*, no. 37 (July-December 1963), Brathwaite observed that 'in the world of Hanuman House, we have the first novel whose basic theme is not rootlessness and the search for social identity; in *A House for Mr. Biswas* we have at last a [West Indian] novel whose central character . . . is really trying to get *in* rather than get *out*' (p. 17). Ramchand, in *The West Indian Novel and Its Background* (London, 1970), takes issue with this: '*A House for Mr. Biswas* I would suggest is the West Indian novel of rootlessness *par excellence*' (p. 192).

The critical concern with images of and models for West Indian society, the sociological bias, is apparent too in one general pattern of response to Naipaul, to be seen both in the critics who stress what they regard as the necessity, accuracy and 'courage' of his image of West Indian society, and in the critics who are careful to point out what to them are the prejudices and distortions which vitiate that image. The concern is also dominant when, for example, Rohlehr says that if he had to compile 'an anthology of current West Indian writing', his first principle would be to try 'as far as possible to determine how far that writing reflected and explored the tensions of the society' (*Bim*, no. 54 (January-June 1972), p. 81).

The concern for the idea of community resolves itself again and again into a concern for the question/problem of language. For Walcott's symbolic West Indian sea-almond trees, 'their leaves' broad dialect' was important because it was 'a coarse,/enduring sound/they shared together' (*The Castaway*, London (1965), p. 37). Gerald Moore sums up the centrality of the critical concern with the question of language when he says, 'The most important of the discoveries made over the intervening thirty years [since the first publication of *Bim*] is that the West Indies has languages of its own'. (See p. 130 below.) Lamming had put the matter differently, but with just as sharp a focus, when in *The Pleasures of Exile* he had said, with a sort of curt defiance, 'English is a West Indian language'. (See p. 25 below.) The drama enacted between Prospero and Caliban is, among other things, and as has been pointed out often enough, a conflict about language. (See, for example, Walcott's 'The Muse of History', below.) What was once a romance between the West Indian writer and the English language became a love-hate relationship. Not surprisingly, the critics are most stimulated to analysis of the language of West Indian writers when that language can be shown to be in some peculiar or essential way West Indian. In any event, the pervasiveness of the agony over language in the following selections is an acute indication of what is to me an insufficiently acknowledged idea—that literature, all literature, is ultimately *about* language.

University of the West Indies,
Jamaica
May 1975

PART I

Contexts for Criticism: General Approaches to the Literature

SYLVIA WYNTER

'The Necessary Background'

... In his long and detailed introduction to *The Islands In Between*, Louis James, as editor, has only this to say about the exile of the West Indian writer:

> Seen against the various tensions of the area, it is not surprising that many creative Caribbean writers moved away from the West Indies to see their predicament in perspective ... V. S. Naipaul — who entitled an account of his visit to his ancestral homeland 'An Area of Darkness' (1964)—and Samuel Selvon left permanently for England. Into exile in London too, went many other creative West Indian writers, including George Lamming, Wilson Harris, Andrew Salkey and Edgar Mittelholzer.

Why does Louis James accept and pass over, as a given fact, a connection without which West Indian writing cannot be properly explained? For James cannot be accused, as W. I. Carr can be, of refusing to see literature in the context of a given time and place. Indeed much of his introduction is given over to a historical sketch of the area which produced West Indian writing; and of the circumstances which helped to define it. Yet this historical sketch is distorted by James's essentially 'branch plant' perspective—a perspective that views the part for the whole; that adjusts new experience to fit an imported model, with a shift here and a shift there; that blinds its horizons in order not to perceive the logical and ultimate connections, that would invalidate the original model that had formed his being and distorted his way of seeing. The 'branch plant' perspective is the perspective of all the 'appeasing arts'; and of their corollary, 'acquiescent criticism'.

What do we mean by this? James does not hesitate to point out the colonial background to West Indian writing. No West Indian, however passionate and anti-colonial, could fault him on this. He says all the right things, makes all the right genuflections. If he praises the British presence in the Caribbean,

> Only an extremist would deny the positive contributions to West Indian social and political life made by England. They are ubiquitous, and deeply ingrained, far more so than in India or

Africa. English education opened up a cultural heritage which reached beyond England to Europe, and Asia and Africa. It provided a highly developed tool of language with which a writer like Walcott could explore his own unique predicament, just as the British liberal traditions formed the basis for the struggle for independence from England.—

Louis James is quick to adjust the balance with this:

At the same time the English traditions could be destructive. Petrified within the social structure as the standards of respectability, they could also, as we have noticed, divide class from class, and constrict the evolution of national ways of life.

If we examine both the praise and the dispraise, we shall find that James has really evaded the issue. He has, to use a just phrase of T. W. Adorno, 'parried by not parrying'. No one, in reading both accounts, could fail to see on which side the balance tilts—in favour of England and her 'positive contributions'. Yet an English education provided Walcott with 'a highly developed tool of language' to explore 'a unique predicament' which England's economic interest had created; a predicament which had profited her. If British liberal traditions formed the basis of the West Indian's struggle for independence, it was the British anti-liberal tradition which, by making him colonial, caused him to have to struggle in the first place. From this long and anti-liberal tradition England also profited. Her 'destructive English traditions' which divided class from class, were there to serve a purpose. To continue an economic and political arrangement which profited her. The more they profited her, the less they profited the West Indies. The end result is an arrangement by which, with independence attained, the majority of the West Indians were illiterate. The writer wanting market and audience had to go to England. As the West Indian University, wanting skilled personnel, had to turn to England. The presence of Louis James in the Caribbean and the absence of the writer in London are part of the same historical process.

The distortion of Louis James's perspective comes from his avoidance of this connection. He sketches the history of the Caribbean from an Archimedean point outside the historical process. Yet it is a process in which he is as involved as is the West Indian. This pretended objectivity and detachment is the common stance of what I call, for convenience, the 'acquiescent critic'. In attempting to write from outside the process, in pretending detachment, the 'acquiescent critic' accepts the status quo, by accepting his own fixed point outside it. He falls into the trap of which Adorno spoke:

He, the cultural critic, speaks as if he represented either unadult-
erated nature or a higher historical stage. Yet his is necessarily of
the same essence as that to which he fancies himself superior.
The insufficiency of the subject ... which passes judgement ...
becomes intolerable when the subject itself is mediated down to
its innermost makeup by the notion to which it opposes itself as
independent and sovereign.

James, as an English teacher teaching in a West Indian university,
passing judgement on West Indian writing, is mediated to his bones
by the colonial experience, by the colonial myth in which he is as
involved, though in a different role, as is the West Indian.

It is Lamming the writer and the West Indian, and not James the
critic and the Englishman, who sees this vital connection. James's
criticism, in the final analysis, is there to reinforce the status quo;
Lamming's is there to question it. Lamming, the questioning critic,
cannot take fixity as his stance; he knows himself and his perspective moulded by a historical process imposed on his being. He
writes from a point of view inside the process. He knows that he
does. Awareness is all. In *The Pleasures of Exile* he begins his
historical sketch of the Caribbean quite differently from James. He
speaks to James, not at him. 'We have met before', Lamming tells
him. 'Four centuries separate our meeting...'

... In *The Pleasures of Exile*, Lamming performs the highest
function of criticism. He *opens* for us Shakespeare's play *The
Tempest*. He reveals extensions of meaning that have hitherto
avoided us. He does this by involving himself, a twentieth-century
Barbadian Negro, within the context of the play. He brings
'immanent criticism' to a new height, that is he reveals the
qualities that the play has as 'an end in itself' by paradoxically
placing it firmly within the context of the adventure of its time.
He says:

> I see *The Tempest* against the background of England's experi-
> ment in colonization ... and it is Shakespeare's capacity for
> experience which leads me to feel that *The Tempest* was also
> prophetic of a political future which is our present.

Lamming places *The Tempest* within the process of England's
creation of Empire. *The Tempest*, he shows us, was as much the
cultural expression of England's adventure as were the voyages of
Drake and Hawkins its economic expression. It is the measure of
Shakespeare's genius that at the height of England-Prospero's
intoxication, he should have been aware of the dimension of
Caliban's tragedy—'That when I waked, I cried to dream once
more'.

It is the measure of Lamming's critical insight that he sees this as the beginning of a *cultural* connection that was not separate from the economic, but lay at its very heart. To elucidate this connection Lamming begins to chart for us 'the triangular course of that tremendous Voyage which swept Caliban from his soil and introduced him to Heaven through the long wet hell of the Middle Passage'. This is the beginning of an African's history as Caliban; and of Hawkins' as Prospero. Both after that voyage had suffered a sea-change and had been transmuted into something terrible and strange. The history of neither Caliban nor Prospero can be understood from now on outside of that relationship.

. . . The West Indian writer is therefore involved in what Fuentes calls 'a daily revolution'. This is the reason for his exile, from Latin America and from here. Prospero's arrangement sees to this. This is, too, in many cases the reason for his failure as novelist, as poet, or what have you. In initiating his revolution, Caliban takes language and tools and concepts from the Prospero whom he must fight. All too often, his writing is accorded, or not accorded, recognition by this very Prospero. All too often, in having to write *for* Prospero's approval, he negates his own intention. The writer needs to write, as Lamming does in *The Pleasures of Exile*, addressing himself to his own audience. That at the same time he addressed himself to Prospero too, is not irrelevant. The relationship with Prospero has not come to [an] end with the physical departure of Prospero. As Lamming acutely realizes, since colonization had been a reciprocal process, decolonization must be equally so. Since it is Prospero who created the myth and assigned the respective roles, the process of demythologization must take place between himself and Caliban. Caliban must, in a dialogue, re-invent, re-define the relation. If Caliban is to become a man, Prospero must cease being a myth of super-man. Once this dialogue has really begun, the historical process which placed Louis James in the Caribbean and Lamming in London can be meaningful.

Lamming, seeing the connection between colonizer and colonized, examined *The Tempest* against the experience of England's early adventure in Empire. Louis James, in spite of the many subsidiary excellencies of his comments, does not see West Indian literature against its necessary background—England's late adventure in the dissolution of Empire. What do we mean by this? For James, unlike Carr, reveals the connection between West Indian writing, the use of dialect etc., and the upsurge, beginning in the thirties, against colonial rule. But he keeps his analysis, with no more than a brief reference, firmly in a West Indian compartment. He does not see West Indian literature as the expression of the breaking out of all the Calibans, not only all over the British Empire, but at the heart of Empire itself . . .

From 'Reflections on West Indian Writing and Criticism', part 1, *Jamaica Journal*, II (December 1968), pp. 23-32 (26-7, 31).

GEORGE LAMMING

The Peasant Roots of the West Indian Novel

... I do not want to make any chauvinistic claim for the West Indian writer. But it is necessary to draw attention to the novelty—not the exotic novelty which inferior colonials and uninformed critics will suggest—but the historic novelty of our situation. We have seen in our lifetime an activity called writing, in the form of the novel, come to fruition without any previous native tradition to draw upon. Mittelholzer and Reid and Selvon and Roger Mais are to the new colonial reader in the West Indies precisely what Fielding and Smollett and the early English novelists would be to the readers of their own generation. These West Indian writers are the earliest pioneers in this method of investigation. They are the first builders of ... a tradition in West Indian imaginative writing: a tradition which will be taken for granted or for the purpose of critical analysis by West Indians of a later generation.

... The education of all these [West Indian] writers is more or less middle-class Western culture, and particularly English culture. But the substance of their books, the general motives and directions, are peasant. One of the most popular complaints made by West Indians against their novelists is the absence of novels about the West Indian middle class.

Why is it that Reid, Mittelholzer in his early work, Selvon, Neville Dawes, Roger Mais, Andrew Salkey, Jan Carew—why is it that their work is shot through and through with the urgency of peasant life? And how has it come about that their colonial education should not have made them pursue the general ambitions of non-provincial writers? How is it that they have not to play at being the Eliots and Henry Jameses of the West Indies? Instead, they move nearer to Mark Twain.

... Unlike the previous governments and departments of educators, unlike the business man importing commodities, the West Indian novelist did not look out across the sea to another source. He looked in and down at what had traditionally been ignored. For the first time the West Indian peasant became other than a cheap source of labour. He became, through the novelist's eye, a living existence, living in silence and joy and fear, involved in riot and carnival. It is the West Indian novel that has restored the West Indian peasant to his true and original status of personality.

... An important question, for the English critic, is not what the West Indian novel has brought to English writing. It would be more correct to ask what the West Indian novelists have contributed to English reading. For the language in which these books are written is English—which, I must repeat—is a West Indian language; and in spite of the unfamiliarity of its rhythms, it remains accessible to the readers of English anywhere in the world. The West Indian contribution to English reading has been made possible by their relation to their themes which are peasant. This is the great difference between the West Indian novelist and the contemporary English novelist.

The English novel from its beginnings to the present exercises in anger has always been middle-class in taste and middle-class by intention. It had to be so. They were all writing for readers who were part of their thing, so to speak. Literacy was and still is seen as a kind of social badge. Today the regiment of illiterates has decreased. More people read in England; and more of them tend to have the same intellectual references. But the badge has changed; and we have the situation where the literate are divided into classes: intellectuals and the rest.

... Writers like Selvon and Vic Reid—key novelists for understanding the literacy and social situation in the West Indies—are essentially peasant. I don't care what jobs they did before; what kind or grade of education they got in their different islands; they never really left the land that once claimed their ancestors like trees. That's a great difference between the West Indian novelist and his contemporary in England. For peasants simply don't respond and see like middle-class people. The peasant tongue has its own rhythms which are Selvon's and Reid's rhythms; and no artifice of technique, no sophisticated gimmicks leading to the mutilation of form, can achieve the specific taste and sound of Selvon's prose.

For this prose is, really, the people's speech, the organic music of the earth. Shakespeare knew that music, and lived at a time when it permeated society. But things have changed beyond belief in England. For the young English novelist, there are really no people. There are only large numbers of dwellers, vagrant or settled vaguely somewhere. Among these there will be a few pockets of individuals who are known through encounter in the same profession, or friendships arrived at through admiration and patronage ... It is not at all by chance that so much of the action of West Indian novels takes place outside, in the open air. This is a long way away from the muted whisper in the living-room cell, or the intellectual stammering which reverberates through the late night coffee caves.

The West Indian who comes near to being an exception to the peasant feel is John Hearne. His key obsession is with an agricultural middle class in Jamaica. I don't want to suggest that this group of people are not a proper subject for fiction; but I've often wondered whether Hearne's theme, with the loaded concern he shows for a mythological, colonial squirearchy, is not responsible for the fact that his work is, at present, less energetic than the West Indian novels at their best. Hearne is a first-class technician, almost perfect within the limitation of conventional story-telling; but the work is weakened, for the langugage is not being *used*, and the Novel as a form is not really being *utilised*. His novels suggest that he has a dread of being identified with the land at peasant level. What he puts into his books is always less interesting than the *omissions* which a careful reader will notice he has forced himself to make. He is not an example of that instinct and root impulse which return the better West Indian writers back to the soil. For soil is a large part of what the West Indian novel has brought back to reading; lumps of earth: unrefined, perhaps, but good, warm, fertile earth.

From *The Pleasures of Exile* (London: Michael Joseph, 1960), pp. 38-9, 44-6.

GORDON ROHLEHR

The Folk in Caribbean Literature

... Like all beginnings [Lamming's] statement[1] was too absolute
and too limiting, especially in the light of the complex little
worlds which West Indian societies are. There are hints that
Lamming himself sensed this. Late in the same work [*The
Pleasures of Exile*], for example, he made distinctions between
the Barbadian, the Trinidadian and the Jamaican ... The different nature of the settlement of the various West Indian islands
has led to differences in temperament, and in response to the
various aspects of West Indian reality, including the question of
relationship to land.

It is possible, for example, that the phenomenal rate of immigra-
tion in nineteenth and early twentieth century Trinidad, and the
recurring problem which that country faced of assimilating
thousands of people of different ethnic backgrounds and languages, have led to what appears to be a general instability and lack of
rooted dedication to the land in the Trinidadian. Yet this statement
would have to be qualified in view of the fact that there is a large
Indian peasantry in Trinidad, who manifest the same pride in and
hunger for land which Lamming mentions as a feature of the
Barbadian and Jamaican peasantries.

There exists, in other words, a difference in outlook between the
town people and the rural dwellers. This is true in varying degrees
for the rest of the West Indies, and the wide range of experiences
treated in West Indian novels makes it clear that the writers are
aware of this. Samuel Selvon writes not only of the Indian
peasantry in Trinidad, but of the rootless drifters, 'smartmen' and
'saga boys' of Port-of-Spain and of people caught somewhere
between the two quite different ways of life. It is a simplification,
therefore, to see him as essentially 'peasant', or as one who 'never
really left the land'.

Similarly, the people of Roger Mais are more normally the
dispossessed of the towns than peasants attached to the land.
Sandwiched in their barrack-houses between the lane and the gully,
they have no land. They are, however, able to reconstruct a
community in spite of the harshness of their milieu and to knit
fragments of communal experience into a single perception of
tragedy, character flowing into character as if the entire group were

a single person. This accounts for the fragmentation of form in *The Hills Were Joyful Together* and for the way Mais contrives to blend the disparate voices and modes into a single weighty philosophising voice. Edward Brathwaite in 'Jazz and the West Indian Novel' makes the same point about Mais's *Brother Man*, comparing Mais's constant alternation between individuals or couples, with jazz improvisations of the twenties and thirties.[2]

Brathwaite sees the West Indies as caught in the same transitional stage between rural and urban existences, which produced the jazzmen of New Orleans in the twenties, and is trying to see whether West Indian writers, in their quest for form, have succeeded in creating the equivalent in verbal organisation to Black American jazz. Not everyone will be able to accept his approach, but it does suggest possible approaches to form and architecture in the West Indian novel, and in the poetry of Edward Brathwaite. Also, it does make it quite clear that the problem in West Indian literature is one of understanding and expressing the flow between rural 'folk' sensibility and experiences of semi- or total urbanisation.

... Lamming's notion of West Indian writers as preoccupied with 'peasant' societies needs to be modified. A more pliable theory is required, one which can accommodate the interplay between country, town and big city, between peasant, artisan and city-slicker or factory worker, and between the ill-defined classes of the West Indies. Also necessary, especially in a complex society such as Trinidad, is a language for describing the really bewildering web of relations in a semi-plural, multi-racial world, and a way of examining the process of creolisation there, which goes beyond the despairing sense of violation and loss, or the sentimental notion of the society as one big happy melting-pot which can teach the world how to celebrate life.

Perhaps Redfield's theory which sees societies as being in a process of movement somewhere along a continuum which extends from the theoretically 'folk' to the theoretically 'urban' can be applied here.[3] It will not cover all the situations possible in the West Indies, but does provide a more flexible theory of society than one which seems to be dividing it into 'peasant', 'middle-class', 'metropolitan', or more broadly still, into 'coloniser' and 'colonised', 'Prospero' and 'Caliban'.

Also in need of qualification is Lamming's notion that the West Indian writers provided a way of seeing the peasant, which for 'the first time' projected him as something 'other than a cheap source of labour'. The supposedly new way of seeing the peasant was, in fact, one of the traditional ways of seeing him, which had been gaining currency since the nineteenth century.

Those who supported the idea of emancipation—and there were

a few historians and commentators who did—wrote of the progress towards a real independence of the former slave. Those who apologised for the plantation system and the planter class, propagated myths of the incredible laziness, stupidity, cowardice, and animality of the Negro in the West Indies. Hence the variety of views expressed by commentators such as Sewell, Underhill, Trollope, Froude, Marlin, Kingsley and J. J. Thomas[4] bore witness to the growing visibility of the peasant as a potential *citizen* of the West Indies. This visibility was to continue, along with the growing debate, most of which centred on problems of education, health, malnutritión and employment.

Thus Sewell, writing in the mid-nineteenth century, was able to depict the peasants as people who were struggling successfully to maintain the spirit of emancipation, and to establish a certain independence from the plantation system:

> Those who are not afraid of the confession will admit that the West Indian Creole has made a good fight. The act of emancipation virtually did no more than place liberty within his reach. Actual independence he had to achieve for himself. All untutored and unqualified as he was, he had to contend against social prejudice, political power, and a gigantic interest, before he could enjoy the boon that the act nominally conferred upon him.[5]

Long before the advent of the West Indian novelist, the peasant was visibly working against tremendous odds towards an essential independence. The presence and 'living existence' of the peasant found its earliest incarnation not in literature, as Lamming claims, but in what the peasant himself had, without benefit of middle-class intellect, been able to build for himself ... As urbanisation increased, the struggle of the peasants against the planter class broadened out into a struggle against whoever were the rulers of the society. This was the reason for the intense political development throughout the West Indies in the years between the two World Wars, which extended into the seminal Guyanese situations of 1952.

It was, therefore, not simply the isolated efforts of the novelists which, in Lamming's words, 'restored the West Indian peasant to his true and original status of personality'. It was the efforts of the West Indian peoples as a whole which provided a dynamic powerful enough to charge the writers of the fifties. These writers *reflected* an awareness which had been there for some time; they could neither *create* nor *restore* what was already present in the creative struggle, rebellion and movement of the West Indian people.

... Edward Brathwaite in his early essays also probed the relationship between the West Indian writer and the 'folk'. At times, his usage of the term 'folk' was as inadequate as Lamming's usage of the term 'peasant'. Indeed, sociologists and anthropologists seem themselves to have been in the throes of a debate as to the viability of the concepts of 'folk' and 'urban', and as to whether they were at all useful for the analysis of social change. In an early article published in *Bim* (No. 25, July-December 1957), 'Sir Galahad and the Islands', Brathwaite indicates a broad contrast between the 'folk' and the 'middle-classes' ....

Brathwaite, while he identifies the 'folk' as the peasants, also speaks of Selvon's '*folk*-sources' as 'the *urban village*'. Here are three concepts: folk, city, and strangest of all, urban village. Yet it is not a simple matter of confusion, because in the West Indies, all possible categories intersect, so that in the midst of a harsh experience in Jamaica, religious cultism flourishes, and identifiably folk genres fertilise the mainstream of urban music. West Indian society is in fluid motion, and often, oscillation, between the two extreme poles of the folk-urban continuum, [which] makes it difficult to define one's terms ...

NOTES

1 See p. 24 above.
2 'Jazz and the West Indian Novel,' *Bim*, Nos 44, 45, 46 (January-May 1967, June-December 1967, January-May 1968). (For Brathwaite's commentary on *Brother Man*, see p. 103 below.)
3 Redfield, R. 'The Folk Society', *American Journal of Sociology,* LII (January 1947).
4 Goveia, E. *A Study of the Historiography of the British West Indies.* Mexico, 1956, Chapter 4.
5 Sewell, W. G. *The Ordeal of Free Labour in the West Indies.* New York, 1861.

From 'The Folk in Caribbean Literature', first instalment, *Tapia* (17 December 1972), pp. 7-8, 13-14 (7-8). (Revised version of a paper presented at the ACLALS conference held at Mona, Jamaica, January 1971.)

WILSON HARRIS

Tradition and the West Indian Novel

I would like first of all to point out that the conventional approach to the 'West Indian' which sees him in crowds—an underprivileged crowd, a happy-go-lucky crowd, a political or a cricketing crowd, a calypso crowd—is one which we have to put aside at this moment for the purposes of our discussion. The status of the West Indian— as a person in world society—is of a much more isolated and problematic character. West Indians in their national context, in their nation-state, as such, are a minority in the world of the twentieth century, a very small minority at that. What in my view is remarkable about the West Indian in depth is a sense of subtle links, the series of subtle and nebulous links which are latent within him, the latent ground of old and new personalities. This is a very difficult view to hold, I grant, because it is not a view which consolidates, which invests in any way in the consolidation of popular character. Rather it seeks to visualize a *fulfilment* of character. Something which is more extraordinary than one can easily imagine. And it is this possible revolution in the novel— *fulfilment* rather than *consolidation*—I would like first of all to look at in a prospective way because I feel it is profoundly consistent with the native tradition—the depth of inarticulate feeling and unrealized wells of emotion belonging to the whole West Indies.

The Potential of the Novel
The consolidation of character is, to a major extent, the preoccupa- tion of most novelists who work in the twentieth century within the framework of the nineteenth-century novel. Indeed the nineteenth- century novel has exercised a very powerful influence on reader and writer alike in the contemporary world. And this is not surprising after all since the rise of the novel in its conventional and historical mould coincides in Europe with states of society which were involved in consolidating their class and other vested interests. As a result 'character' in the novel rests more or less on the self-sufficient individual—on elements of 'persuasion' (a refined or liberal persuasion at best in the spirit of the philosopher Whitehead) rather then 'dialogue' or 'dialectic' in the profound and unpredictable sense of person which Martin Buber, for example, evokes. The

novel of persuasion rests on grounds of apparent common sense: a certain 'selection' is made by the writer, the selection of items, manners, uniform conversation, historical situations, etc. all lending themselves to build and present an individual span of life which yields self-conscious and fashionable judgements, self-conscious and fashionable moralities. The tension which emerges is the tension of individuals—great or small—on an accepted plane of society we are persuaded has an inevitable existence. There is an element of freedom in this method nevertheless, an apparent range of choices, but I believe myself that this freedom—in the convention which distinguishes it, however liberal this may appear—is an illusion. It is true of course that certain kinds of realism, impressive realism, and also a kind of fateful honesty distinguished and still distinguish the novel of individual character especially where an element of great suffering arises and does a kind of spiritual violence to every 'given' conception .... I would like to break off here for a moment to say that the novel of the West Indies, the novel written by West Indians of the West Indies (or of other places for that matter), belongs—in the main—to the conventional mould. Which is not surprising at this stage since the novel which consolidates situations to depict protest or affirmation is consistent with most kinds of over-riding advertisement and persuasion upon the writer for him to make national and political and social simplifications of experience in the world at large today. Therefore the West Indian novel—so-called—in the main—is inclined to suffer in depth (to lose in depth) and may be properly assessed in nearly every case in terms of surface tension and realism—as most novels are assessed today—in the perceptive range of choices which emerges, and above all in the way in which the author *persuades* you to ally yourself with situation and character .... I believe it is becoming possible to see even now at this relatively early time that the ruling and popular convention, as such, is academic and provincial in the light of a genuine—and if I may use a much abused term—*native* tradition of depth.

Native and Phenomenal Environment
The native and phenomenal environment of the West Indies, as I see it, is broken into many stages in the way in which one surveys an existing river in its present bed while plotting at the same time ancient and abandoned, indeterminate courses the river once followed. When I speak of the West Indies I am thinking of overlapping contexts of Central and South America as well. For the mainstream of the West Indies in my estimation possesses an enormous escarpment down which it falls, and I am thinking here of the European discovery of the New World and conquest of the ancient American civilizations which were themselves related by

earlier and obscure levels of conquest. This escarpment seen from another angle possesses the features of a watershed, main or subsidiary, depending again on how one looks at it.

The environment of the Caribbean is steeped—as I said before—in such broken conceptions as well as misconceptions of the residue and meaning of conquest. No wonder in the jungles of Guiana and Brazil, for example, material structural witnesses may be obliterated or seem to exist in a terrible void of unreality. Let us look once again at the main distinction which for convenience one may describe as the divide pre-Columbian/post-Columbian. The question is—how can one begin to reconcile the broken parts of such an enormous heritage, especially when those broken parts appear very often like a grotesque series of adventures, volcanic in its precipitate effects as well as human in its vulnerable settlement? This distinction is a large, a very large one which obviously has to be broken down into numerous modern tributaries and other immigrant movements and distinctions so that the smallest area one envisages, island or village, prominent ridge or buried valley, flatland or heartland, is charged immediately with the openness of imagination, and the longest chain of sovereign territories one sees is ultimately no stronger than its weakest and most obscure connecting link.

Vision of Consciousness

It is in this light that one must seek to relate the existing pattern of each community to its variable past, and if I may point to the phenomenal divide again, the question which arises is how one can begin to let these parts act on each other in a manner which fulfils *in the person* the most nebulous instinct for a vocation of being and independent spirit within a massive landscape of apparent lifelessness which yields nevertheless the essential denigration and erosion of historical perspectives. This indeed is a peculiarly West Indian question, strange as it may appear to some, and in fact a question peculiar to every phenomenal society where minorities (frail in historical origin or present purpose) may exist, and where comparatively new immigrant and racial cells sometimes find themselves placed within a dangerous misconception and upon a reactionary treadmill. And it is right here—if one begins to envisage an expanding outward and inward creative significance for the novel —that the monument of consolidation breaks down and becomes the need for a vision of consciousness. And this vision of consciousness is the peculiar reality of language because the concept of language is one which continuously transforms inner and outer formal categories of experience, earlier and representative modes of speech itself, the still life resident in painting and sculpture as such, even music which one ceases to 'hear'—the peculiar reality of language provides a medium to *see* in consciousness the 'free' motion and to *hear* with consciousness the 'silent' flood of sound by a continuous inward revisionary and momentous logic of potent explosive images evoked in the mind. Such a capacity for language is a real and necessary one in a world where the inarticulate person is continuously frozen or legislated for in mass and a genuine experience of his distress, the instinct of distress, sinks into a void. The nightmare proportions of this are already becoming apparent throughout the world.

The point I want to make in regard to the West Indies is that the pursuit of a strange and subtle goal, melting pot, call it what you like, is the mainstream (though unacknowledged) tradition in the Americas. And the significance of this is akin to the European preoccupation with alchemy, with the growth of experimental science, the poetry of science as well as of explosive nature which is informed by a solution of images, agnostic humility and essential beauty, rather than vested interest in a fixed assumption and classification of things.

Let us look at the *individual* African slave. I say *individual* deliberately though this is an obviously absurd label to apply to the persons of slaves in their binding historical context. But since their arrival in the Americas bred a new and painful obscure isolation (which is difficult to penetrate in any other terms but a free conceptual imagination) one may perhaps dream to visualize the suffering and original grassroots of individuality. (In fact I believe this is one of the growing points of both alienation and feeling in modern West Indian literature.) He (the problematic slave) found himself spiritually alone since he worked side by side with others who spoke different dialects. The creative human consol- ation—if one dwells upon it meaningfully today—lies in the search for a kind of inward dialogue and space when one is deprived of a ready conversational tongue and hackneyed comfortable approach.

Irony

I would like to stress again the curious irony involved in this. To assume that the slave was an *individual* is historically absurd since the *individual* possesses certain distinguishing marks, education, status, background, morality, etc., while a slave—in the American context of which we are speaking, as in most situations I imagine— was like an animal put up for sale. (The same qualitative depriva- tion—though not in terms of absolute coercion—exists for the illiterate East Indian peasant, for example, in the twentieth century in the West Indies.) When therefore one speaks of an inarticulate body of men, confined on some historical plane, as possessing the grassroots of Western individuality one is creatively rejecting, as if it were an illusion, every given, total and self-sufficient situation and dwelling within a capacity for liberation, a capacity for mental and unpredictable pain which the human person endured *then* or endures now *in* or *for* any time or place. To develop the point further, it is clear that one is rejecting the sovereign individual as such. For in spite of his emancipation he consolidates every advance by conditioning himself to function solely within his contemporary situation more or less as the slave appears bound still upon his historical and archaic plane. It is in this 'closed' sense that freedom becomes a progressive illusion and it is within the open capacity of the person—as distinct from the persuasive refinements of any social order—within the suffering and enduring mental capacity of the obscure person (which capacity one shares with both 'collective' slave and 'separate' individual in the past and in the future) that a scale emerges and continues indefinitely to emerge which makes it possible for *one* (whoever that *one* may be, today or tomorrow) to measure and abolish each given situation.

Scale
The use of the word 'scale' is important, a scale or a ladder, because bear in mind what we are saying is that the capacity of the person in terms of words and images is associated with a drama of living consciousness, a drama within which one responds not only to the overpowering and salient features of a plane of existence (which 'over-poweringness', after all, is often a kind of self-indulgent realism) but to the essence of life, to the instinctive grains of life which continue striving and working in the imagination for fulfilment, a visionary character of fulfilment. Such a fulfilment can never be intellectually imposed on the material; it can only be realized in experiment instinctive to the native life and passion of persons known and unknown in a structure of time and space.

Therefore it is clear that the change which is occurring slowly within the novel and the play and the poem is one which has been maturing slowly for centuries. Some of the most daring intimations exist in the works of modern writers, Proust, Joyce, Faulkner, and I would also venture to say in the peculiar style and energy of Australian novelists like Patrick White and Hal Porter, a French novelist like Claude Simon, and English/Canadian novelist like Malcolm Lowry and an African problematic writer like Tutuola. Lowry's novel *Under the Volcano* is set in Mexico where it achieves a tragic reversal of the material climate of our time, assisted by residual images, landscape as well as the melting pot of history, instinctive to the cultural environment of the Central and South Americas.

Let us apply our scale, for example, to the open myth of El

Dorado. The religious and economic thirst for exploration was true
of the Spanish conquistador, of the Portuguese, French, Dutch and
English, of Raleigh, of Fawcett, and it is true of the black modern
pork-knocker and the pork-knocker of all races. An instinctive
idealism associated with this adventure was overpowered within
individual and collective by enormous greed, cruelty and exploitation. In fact it would have been very difficult a century ago to
present these exploits as other than a very material and degrading
hunger for wealth spiced by a kind of self-righteous spirituality. It
is difficult enough today within clouds of prejudice and nihilism;
nevertheless the substance of this adventure, involving men of all
races, past and present conditions, has begun to acquire a residual
pattern of illuminating correspondences. El Dorado, City of Gold,
City of God, grotesque, unique coincidence, another window
within upon the Universe, another drunken boat, another ocean,
another river; in terms of the novel the distribution of a frail
moment of illuminating adjustments within a long succession and
grotesque series of adventures, past and present, capable *now* of
discovering themselves and continuing to discover themselves so
that in one sense one relives and reverses the 'given' conditions of
the past, freeing oneself from catastrophic idolatry and blindness
to one's own historical and philosophical concepts and misconceptions which may bind one within a statuesque present or a false
future. Humility is all, says the poet, humility is endless.

  . . . [I]t seems to me vital—in a time when it is easy to succumb to
fashionable tyrannies or optimisms—to break away from the
conception so many people entertain that literature is an extension
of a social order or a political platform. In fact it is one of the
ironic things with West Indians of my generation that they may
conceive of themselves in the most radical political light but their
approach to art and literature is one which consolidates the most
conventional and documentary techniques in the novel. In fact
many of the great Victorians—Ruskin, Gerard Manley Hopkins,
Dickens in *Bleak House* for example, where a strange kinship
emerges with the symbolism of both Poe and Kafka—are revolu-
tionaries who make the protestations of many a contemporary
radical look like a sham and a pose. The fact is—even when
sincerely held, political radicalism is merely a fashionable attitude
unless it is accompanied by profound insights into the experimental
nature of the arts and the sciences. There are critics who claim that
the literary revolution of the first half of the twentieth century may
well stem from the work of Pound and Eliot, Joyce and Wyndham
Lewis. I am not prepared to go into this claim now but the point
is—how is it that figures such as these, described in some quarters
as conservative, remain 'explosive' while many a fashionable rebel
grows to be superficial and opportunistic?

Literature has a bearing on society, yes, a profound and imaginative bearing wherein the life of tradition in all its complexity gives a unique value to the life of vocation in society, whether that vocation happens to be in science, in education, in the study of law or in the dedicated craft of one's true nature and life. For if tradition were dogma it would be entirely dormant and passive but since it is inherently active at all times, whether secretly or openly, it participates [in] the ground of living necessity by questioning and evaluating all assumptions of character and conceptions of place or destiny. A scale of distinctions emerges, distinctions which give the imagination room to perceive the shifting border line between original substance and vicarious hollow, the much advertised rich and the hackneyed caricature of the poor, the overfed body of illusion and the underfed stomach of reality—room to perceive also overlapping areas of invention and creation, the hair-spring experiment of crucial illumination which divides the original spiritual germ of an idea from its musing plastic development and mature body of expression. It is this kind of scale which is vital to the life of the growing person in society. And this scale exists in a capacity for imagination. A scale which no one can impose since to do so is to falsify the depth of creative experience, the growth and feeling for creative experience.

It is a scale which at certain moments realizes itself in a range and capacity which are phenomenal—the peaks of tragedy, of epic, of myth have been such moments in the dialogue of culture and civilization—while at other times we must be grateful if we are allowed to work at the humility of our task with all of our creative suffering instincts, leaving ourselves open, as it were, to vision . . . .

From 'Tradition and the West Indian Novel', in *Tradition, the Writer and Society* (London and Port-of-Spain: New Beacon, 1967), pp. 28-47 (28-36, 45-7).

DEREK WALCOTT

The Muse of History

> *History is the nightmare from which*
> *I am trying to awake.*
> Joyce

I

The common experience of the New World, even for its patrician writers whose veneration of the Old is read as the idolatry of the mestizo, is colonialism. They too are victims of tradition, but they remind us of our debt to the great dead, that those who break a tradition first hold it in awe. They perversely encourage disfavour, but because their sense of the past is of a timeless, yet habitable, moment, the New World owes them more than it does those who wrestle with that past, for their veneration subtilises an arrogance which is tougher than violent rejection. They know that by openly fighting tradition we perpetuate it, that revolutionary literature is a filial impulse, and that maturity is the assimilation of the features of every ancestor.

When these writers cunningly describe themselves as classicists and pretend an indifference to change, it is with an irony as true of the colonial anguish as the fury of the radical. If they appear to be phony aristocrats, it is because they have gone past the confrontation of history, that Medusa of the New World.

These writers reject the idea of history as time for its original concept as myth, the partial recall of the race. For them history is fiction, subject to a fitful muse, memory. Their philosophy, based on a contempt for historic time, is revolutionary, for what they repeat to the New World is its simultaneity with the Old. Their vision of man is elemental, a being inhabited by presences, not a creature chained to his past. Yet the method by which we are taught the past, the progress from motive to event, is the same by which we read narrative fiction. In time every event becomes an exertion of memory and is thus subject to invention. The further the facts, the more history petrifies into myth. Thus, as we grow older as a race, we grow aware that history is written, that it is a kind of literature without morality, that in its actuaries the ego of the race is indissoluble and that everything depends on whether we write this fiction through the memory of hero or of victim.

In the New World servitude to the muse of history has produced a literature of recrimination and despair, a literature of revenge written by the descendants of slaves or a literature of remorse written by the descendants of masters. Because this literature serves historical truth, it yellows into polemic or evaporates in pathos. The truly tough aesthetic of the New World neither explains nor forgives history. It refuses to recognise it as a creative or culpable force. This shame and awe of history possess poets of the Third World who think of language as enslavement and who, in a rage for identity, respect only incoherence or nostalgia.

II

The great poets of the New World, from Whitman to Neruda, reject this sense of history. Their vision of man in the New World is Adamic. In their exuberance he is still capable of enormous wonder. Yet he has paid his accounts to Greece and Rome and walks in a world without monuments and ruins. They exhort him against the fearful magnet of older civilisations. Even in Borges, where the genius seems secretive, immured from change, it celebrates an elation which is vulgar and abrupt, the life of the plains given an instant archaism by the hieratic style. Violence is felt with the simultaneity of history. So the death of a gaucho does not merely repeat, but is, the death of Caesar. Fact evaporates into myth. This is not the jaded cynicism which sees nothing new under the sun, it is an elation which sees everything as renewed. Like Borges too, the poet St-John Perse conducts us from the mythology of the past to the present without a tremor of adjustment. This is the revolutionary spirit at its deepest, it recalls the spirit to arms. In Perse there is the greatest width of elemental praise of winds, seas, rains. The revolutionary or cyclic vision is as deeply rooted as the patrician syntax. What Perse glorifies is not veneration but the perennial freedom; his hero remains the wanderer, the man who moves through the ruins of great civilisations with all his worldly goods by caravan or pack mule, the poet carrying entire cultures in his head, bitter perhaps, but unencumbered. His are poems of massive or solitary migrations through the elements. They are the same in spirit as the poems of Whitman or Neruda, for they seek spaces where praise of the earth is ancestral.

III

New World poets who see the 'classic style' as stasis must see it also as historical degradation, rejecting it as the language of the master.

This self-torture arises when the poet also sees history as language, when he limits his memory to the suffering of the victim. Their admirable wish to honour the degraded ancestor limits their language to phonetic pain, the groan of suffering, the curse of revenge. The tone of the past becomes an unbearable burden, for they must abuse the master or hero in his own language, and this implies self-deceit. Their view of Caliban is of the enraged pupil. They cannot separate the rage of Caliban from the beauty of his speech when the speeches of Caliban are equal in their elemental power to those of his tutor. The language of the torturer mastered by the victim. This is viewed as servitude, not as victory.

But who in the New World does not have a horror of the past, whether his ancestor was torturer or victim? Who, in the depth of conscience, is not silently screaming for pardon or for revenge? The pulse of New World history is the racing pulse beat of fear, the tiring cycles of stupidity and greed. The tongues above our prayers utter the pain of entire races to the darkness of a Manichean God: *Dominus illuminatio mea*, for what was brought to this New World under the guise of divine light, the light of the sword blade and the light of *Dominus illuminatio mea*, was the same irridescent serpent brought by a contaminating Adam, the same tortured Christ exhibited with Christian exhaustion, but what was also brought in the seeded entrails of the slave was a new nothing, a darkness which intensified the old faith.

In time the slave surrendered to amnesia. That amnesia is the true history of the New World. That is our inheritance, but to try and understand why this happened, to condemn or justify is also the method of history, and these explanations are always the same: This happened because of that, this was understandable because, and in those days men were such. These recriminations exchanged, the contrition of the master replaces the vengeance of the slave, and here colonial literature is most pietistic, for it can accuse great art of feudalism and excuse poor art as suffering. To radical poets poetry seems the homage of resignation, an essential fatalism. But it is not the pressure of the past which torments great poets but the weight of the present:

> there are so many dead,
> and so many dikes the red sun breached,
> and so many heads battering hulls
> and so many hands that have closed over kisses
> and so many things that I want to forget.
>
> *Neruda*

The sense of history in poets lives rawly along their nerves:

> My land without name, without America,
> equinoctial stamen, lance-like purple,

your aroma rose through my roots
into the cut I drained, into the most tenuous
word not yet born in my mouth.

Neruda

It is this awe of the numinous, this elemental privilege of naming the New World which annihilates history in our great poets, an elation common to all of them, whether they are aligned by heritage to Crusoe and Prospero or to Friday and Caliban. They reject ethnic ancestry for faith in elemental man. The vision, the 'democratic vista', is not metaphorical, it is a social necessity. A political philosophy rooted in elation would have to accept belief in a second Adam, the re-creation of the entire order, from religion to the simplest domestic rituals. The myth of the noble savage would not be revived, for that myth never emanated from the savage but has always been the nostalgia of the Old World, its longing for innocence. The great poetry of the New World does not pretend to such innocence, its vision is not naïve. Rather, like its fruits, its savour is a mixture of the acid and the sweet, the apples of its second Eden have the tartness of experience. In such poetry there is a bitter memory and it is the bitterness that dries last on the tongue. It is the acidulous that supplies its energy. The golden apples of this sun are shot with acid. The taste of Neruda is citric, the *Pomme de Cythère* of Césaire sets the teeth on edge, the savour of Perse is of salt fruit at the sea's edge, the sea grape, the 'fat-poke', the sea almond. For us in the archipelago the tribal memory is salted with the bitter memory of migration.

To such survivors, to all the decimated tribes of the New World who did not suffer extinction, their degraded arrival must be seen as the beginning, not the end of our history. The shipwrecks of Crusoe and of the crew in *The Tempest* are the end of an Old World. It should matter nothing to the New World if the Old is again determined to blow itself up, for an obsession with progress is not within the psyche of the recently enslaved. That is the bitter secret of the apple. The vision of progress is the rational madness of history seen as sequential time, of a dominated future. Its imagery is absurd. In the history books the discoverer sets a shod foot on virgin sand, kneels, and the savage also kneels from his bushes in awe. Such images are stamped on the colonial memory, such heresy as the world's becoming holy from Crusoe's footprint or the imprint of Columbus' knee. These blasphemous images fade, because these hieroglyphs of progress are basically comic. And if the idea of the New and the Old becomes increasingly absurd, what must happen to our sense of time, what else can happen to history itself, but that it too is becoming absurd? This is not existentialism. Adamic, elemental man cannot be existential.

His first impulse is not self-indulgence but awe, and existentialism is simply the myth of the noble savage gone baroque. Such philosophies of freedom are born in cities. Existentialism is as much nostalgia as is Rousseau's sophisticated primitivism, as sick a recurrence in French thought as the isle of Cythera, whether it is the tubercular, fevered imagery of Watteau or the same fever turned delirious in Rimbaud and Baudelaire. The poets of the 'new Aegean', of the Isles of the Blest, the Fortunate Isles, of the remote Bermudas, of Prospero's isle, of Crusoe's Juan Fernandez, of Cythera, of all those rocks named like the beads of a chaplet, they know that the old vision of paradise wrecks here.

> I want to hear a song in which the rainbow breaks
> and the curlew alights among forgotten shores
> I want the liana creeping on the palm-tree
> (on the trunk of the present 'tis our stubborn future)
> I want the conquistador with unsealed armour
> lying down in death of perfumed flowers,
> the foam censing a sword gone rusty
> in the pure blue flight of slow wild cactuses
>
> *Césaire*

But to most writers of the archipelago who contemplate only the shipwreck, the New World offers not elation but cynicism, a despair at the vices of the Old which they feel must be repeated. Their malaise is an oceanic nostalgia for the older culture and a melancholy at the new, and this can go as deep as a rejection of the untamed landscape, a yearning for ruins. To such writers the death of civilisations is architectural, not spiritual, seeded in their memories is an imagery of vines ascending broken columns, of dead terraces, of Europe as a nourishing museum. They believe in the responsibility of tradition, but what they are in awe of is not tradition, which is alert, alive, simultaneous, but of history, and the same is true of the new magnifiers of Africa. For these their deepest loss is of the old gods, the fear that it is worship which has enslaved progress. Thus the humanism of politics replaces religion. They see such gods as part of the process of history, subjected like the tribe to cycles of achievement and despair. Because the Old World concept of God is anthropomorphic, the New World slave was forced to remake himself in His image, despite such phrases as 'God is light, and in Him is no darkness', and at this point of intersecting faiths the enslaved poet and enslaved priest surrendered their power. But the tribe in bondage learned to fortify itself by cunning assimilation of the religion of the Old World. What seemed to be surrender was redemption. What seemed the loss of tradition was its renewal. What seemed the death of faith was its rebirth. . . .

From 'The Muse of History', in Orde Coombs (ed.), *Is Massa Day Dead?* (New York, Anchor Press/Doubleday, 1974), pp. 1-27 (1-7).

PART II

From Colonialism to Independence

NGUGI WA THIONG'O

George Lamming's *In the Castle of My Skin*

It will be our argument that although it is set in a village in a period well before any of the West Indian islands had achieved independence, *In the Castle of My Skin* (New York, 1954) is a study of a colonial revolt; that it shows the motive forces behind it and its development through three main stages: a static phase, then a phase of rebellion, ending in a phase of achievement and disillusionment with society poised on the edge of a new struggle; that it sharply delineates the opposition between the aspirations of the peasantry and those of the emergent native élite, an opposition which, masked in the second phase, becomes clear during the stage of apparent achievement. The novel itself is built on a three-tier time structure corresponding broadly to our three stages: the first three chapters describe stable life, a village community whose social consciousness is limited to a struggle with immediate nature; the next six chapters deal with a village whose consciousness is awakened into a wider vision, involving challenge of and struggle against the accepted order of things; while the last chapters show the ironic dénouement; a new class of native lawyers, merchants, teachers has further displaced the peasantry from the land. But underlying the story's progress in time is a general conception of human history as a movement from the state of nature to a 'higher' consciousness; it is a movement from relative stability in a rural culture to a state of alienation, strife and uncertainty in the modern world.

The restless note is struck at the very beginning: looking at the rain, the hero can see the raindrops in terms of his interior life: 'our lives—meaning our fears and their corresponding ideals—seemed to escape down an imaginary drain that was our future' (p. 2). The image anticipates the end, where the boy now about to embark on an adult's world away from home casts a last glance behind him:

> The earth where I walked was a marvel of blackness and I knew
> in a sense more deep than simple departure I had said farewell,
> farewell to the land. (p. 312)

The words—note the finality and a wistful remembrance in the tone—sum up what has happened: not only the boy's childhood but an organic way of life has ended; the village has also embarked on an uncertain future. What is this organic life, and what are the forces disturbing it?

... The villagers, numbering about three thousand, live in what is, essentially, a feudal society. At the head of the Estate is Creighton, whose house appropriately stands on a hill, dominating all below it. The overseers, the police constables and the school teachers make the middle stratum. At the bottom of this social hierarchy are the peasants, who over the years have acquired customary rights to their homes and plots of land. They accept the social order as divinely willed and dwell under the shadow of Creighton's paternal benevolence. Wealth, law and police power have combined in varying degrees to enforce this acceptance, and produce in the mind of the villagers the idea of the great; subservient complexes govern their every response to and contact with Creighton. What distinguishes Creighton Estate from earlier forms of feudalism, more highly stratified with corresponding duties and rights, is its colonial setting with roots in slavery. The rights and duties are divinely willed by Creighton and Great Britain. The very educational system deliberately aims at buttressing the attitude of acceptance .... The only history which they have been taught is that of Britain.

> They had read about the Battle of Hastings and William the Conqueror. That happened so many hundred years ago. And slavery was thousands of years before that. It was too far back for anyone to worry about teaching it as history. That's really why it wasn't taught. (p. 52)

Lamming evokes the confusion in the minds of the boys as they puzzle out a phenomenon they can't understand. At times they don't even believe it happened, or else explain issues of freedom and slavery in terms of biblical mythology .... The Queen's birthday and the whole educational apparatus at Groddeck's Boys School ... is used to encourage the myth of Barbados being little England. The boys' restless minds find the evasive answer of the older people and the teachers inadequate. What is slavery? What is freedom? Curious, puzzled and pained, the boys turn to religion for an answer. The Christian view of man (Make me a captive, Lord, and then I shall be free) seems to offer a meaningful explanation. Since the boys belong to a new generation that has no direct experience of slavery, and yet have no book knowledge of their immediate past, they seek to find their roots in a general human predicament of sin, death, resurrection and salvation by grace. Even more important for our argument, we are shown how they see this grace as lying somewhere in the Empire. Imperialism and colonialism become sanctified by Christian grace. And all this seems to point in one direction: subservience and acceptance.

But Lamming shows how the seeds of crisis already exist within the present order. Fear and antagonism rule the relationships between people in different social scales. The landlord might at first appear a god whose eminence and dominance is not to be questioned: whenever his son, for instance, passes through the village, the peasants move back, and he gives the order. He makes no demands, or few, we are told, but merely accepts a privilege they offer. There may be a silent protest, but no one is really angry—'acceptance is all'. True, but people's fear and hatred are turned, not against the landlord directly, but against his middlemen: the overseers and the constables. To the villagers the overseer is the enemy. And to the overseer, the villagers are the enemy, 'the low-down nigger people because they couldn't bear to see one of their kind get along without feeling envy and hate'. At least that is what he thinks is the motive force behind their occasional refusal to obey his orders. The overseer walks on a tightrope of fear and insecurity: his enemy, 'my people', might at any time do something which would arouse Creighton's wrath; his privileged position is in constant jeopardy because it depends on the unpredictable will of the white people. He and the constable and the schoolteacher are the forerunners of the colonial bourgeoisie who co-operate with the white man and even share the oppressor's view of the peasants and workers. Rejected in the social world of the white rulers and alienated from the masses by their jobs and education, they turn their frustration inward, against themselves, or else vent it on their own people.

> If the low-down nigger people weren't what they are, the others couldn't say anything about us. Suspicion, distrust, hostility. These operated in every decision. You never can tell with my people. It was the language of the lawyers and doctors who had returned stamped like an envelope with what they called the culture of the Mother Country. (p. 19)

And yet it is from the ranks of the elite, precisely because they are better placed to articulate their desires and discontent, that you get the leaders of colonial revolt. In *In the Castle of My Skin* it is a dismissed schoolteacher, Mr Slime, who exploits and directs the village's collective consciousness into an instrument of challenge and change.

In the process of change, Mr Slime functions as a catalyst which releases the developing conflicts in society. Like Marcus Garvey, who from the moment he came down 'an' tells us that the Lord ain't going to drop manna in we mouths I start to think', Mr Slime kindles in them a dream ('he speak the other night how he goin' to make us owners o' this land . . . I couldn't sort of catch my breath when I hear it, but 'tis a big thing to expect . . .'), which makes them look differently at the hitherto existing relations on the Estate. It occurs to them, for instance, that the landlord is as much dependent on them, the village, their labour, as they on him.

> ' 'Tis true,' said Mr Forster, 'you couldn't have the land without the village.'
> 'And he can't do without the village either,' said the overseer's brother.
> 'He couldn't feel as happy anywhere else in this God's world than he feel on that said same hill lookin' down at us.' (p. 95)

Because of the new mood, they haul Creighton down from God's heaven on the hill and reduce him to human proportions, on the Estate: hence they can now look at him consciously and critically, rejecting for instance his paternalism, or seeing his humanitarianism for what it really is:

> He's a nice sort of man, the landlord; he kind, he will give you if he think you really need, he's really like that, but if he got to spend any r'al sum of money, it give him heart failure. And he got more than he could ever spend in this God's world. (p. 94)

A privileged minority is the most charitable and humanitarian in any society: they possess God's own benevolence and regulate their relationship with the lower orders from Olympian heights, carrying themselves with divine aloofness. They must avoid contact, must never assume human flesh, for to be human, Lamming tells us in another beautifully realised episode involving the boys and a fisherman, is to be vulnerable. It is in this context that Creighton's anger and pain are understandable once the people not only reject his paternalism but actually show, or seem to show, disrespect to his person. Instinctively, he realises that any personal disrespect is a challenge to the value-system that legitimises his power over the people:

> He [the landlord] say to me sittin' in the sun beside the heap o' hay, he says we won't ever understand the kind o' responsibility he feel for you an' me an' the whole village. He say it was a real responsibility. There ain't much he can do whatever anybody may say, but he'd always feel that responsibility. We ain't his children he say, but the feelin' wus something like that. He had

sort o' take care o' those who belong to the village. Things wus never as they should be, he say. He know that full well. But nothin' take away that feelin' o' responsibility he feel for you an' me an' all o' we here in this corner o' God's earth. An he say we wus lucky 'cause there be some in this islan' who never knew anybody to feel that kind of responsibility for them.

Ma, who has sympathy for the landlord and is pained by the current mood of disrespect, had gone to see him to apologise for her people's sacrilege. She is old and religious, and she is resigned to the *status quo*. She distrusts violent changes, and the future anyway is always dark and unpredictable. But her husband, Pa, infected with the new mood, rejects his wife's cautionary tale. It is Pa, gropingly, puzzled, but welcoming the new dream, who best summarises the prevailing thoughts and attitudes:

I ain't know exact, Ma, an' Mr Slime never so much as say except that he feel that you an' all the rest who been here donkeys years, 'tis time that we own it. If Mr Creighton an' all the Creightons from time past can own it, there ain't no reason why we mustn't. (p. 84)

This is a revolutionary thought: what it calls for is a total overhaul of all the relations hitherto governing the island—the colonial plantocracy. Not surprisingly, some people are frightened: Ma in her religious reverence for life and continuous order, instinctively perceives the suffering attending any revolutionary changes; she fears for the children, 'the young that comin' up so fast to take the place of the old'. But most of the villagers, even when they are nervous at the daring of their own thoughts, are mesmerised by the possibilities for them and their children. Mr Slime has gained their confidence, not merely by kindling a dream where there was a vacuum, but by actually pointing at a concrete agency: a Friendly Society and a Penny Bank, which has grown in strength over a year, has shown them what their united action can achieve. The achievement of Mr Slime is this: he has given the people a measure of self-respect, a new estimation of their own worth; arising from the self-confidence regained, their imagination and thoughts rage, and like flames, reach out for other accepted notions in religion and eduation.

In *In the Castle of My Skin* Christianity, juxtaposed with Nature and with natural, healthy relationships between people, is seen as disrupting peoples' lives. Sometimes this brings about comic situations like that of Jan, Jen, and Susie.

. . . But apart from its destructive effects on individual lives, Lamming shows us how Christian values legitimize colonial

authority, spiritually emasculating a whole community. A rejection
of Creighton's domination is hence preceded by a questioning
rejection of religion and Christian teachings:

> They turn us dotish with all these nancy stories 'bout born again,
> an' we never ever give ourself a chance to get up an' get. Nothin'
> ain't goin' change here til we sort o' stop payin' notice to that
> sort o' joke 'bout a old man goin' born again. It ain't only
> stupid but it sound kind o' nasty, an' that's what Mr Slime want
> to put an end to. He mention that said same thing last night in
> the speech. An' he call it tomfoolery. 'Tis what got us as we is,
> he say. (p. 136)

Not only Christianity. The shoemaker and his friends now question
the kind of education Lamming depicts in the first section of the
novel. But they can only grope in the dark slowly. Some, like the
shoemaker, who have read bits from newspapers, can just begin to
glimpse at the connection between education and power and try to
pass on the knowledge to their ignorant brethren. When Forster
and Bob's father, for instance, argue that Barbados has the best
education,

> 'But if you look good,' said the shoemaker 'if you remember
> good, you'll never remember that they ever tell us 'bout Marcus
> Garvey. They never even tell us that they wus a place where we
> live call Africa. An' the night that he spoke there in the Queen's
> Park an' elsewhere, I see a certain teacher in that said high
> school walk from the meeting.'
> 'Why he walk out for?'
> ' 'Cause he didn't like Garvey tellin' him 'bout he's any
> brother,' the overseer's brother said . . .
> ' 'Tain't no joke,' the shoemaker said, 'if you tell half of them
> that work in those places they have something to do with Africa
> they's piss straight in your face.'
> 'But why you goin' to tell men that for,' said Mr Forster, 'why
> tell a man he's somebody brother when he ain't?'
> 'That's what I mean,' the shoemaker said, 'that's just what
> I mean.'

That these things are being discussed at the market square where
before men met to discuss gossip from across the road is itself a
sign of the change that demands even more changes.

Two views of change run side by side in their awakened
consciousness: some, like the shoemaker, see change as an eternal
theme of nature and hence inescapable; the community should
therefore ally itself with the positive forces, for 'if times goes on

changin', changin', an' we here don't make a change one way
or the next, 'tis simply a matter that times will go along 'bout it
business an' leave we all here still waitin'.' Even their knowledge
of history, albeit limited, seems to prove their point: there was once
Alexander the Great; where is he now? Then there was Caesar and
the 'great big' Roman Empire, the Portuguese and Spanish colonial
empires; these too had eventually crumbled. In the same way, the
British Empire would surely collapse:

> God don't like ugly, an' whenever these big great empires starts
> to get ugly with thing they does the Almighty puts his hand down
> once an' for all. He tell them without talkin', fellows, you had
> your day. (p. 100)

There are others who argue differently. To them, all convolutions
of history are mere superficialities. When Pa becomes enthusiastic
over Mr Slime's schemes of emigration to America, Ma reminds
him of his (Pa's) emigration to Panama, and his present still poor
circumstances. In the same way, the present generation will go to
America and come back 'an' they'll sit under the lamp-post an'
say night after night what an' what they use to do'. It will be
different, argues Pa, for in America money flows faster than the
flood. She counters

> 'Twill be the same all over again, Pa. Money come an' money go,
> an' 'tis a thing that move through yuh fingers as the said same
> water you talk about. (p. 83)

Mr Slime's strength lies in his ability to harmonize these warring
views into a vision embodying people's deepest aspirations. To the
villagers he is a new Moses leading them to a Jerusalem where they
can have better houses and permanently own their plots of land;
hence they are ready to endure thirst and hunger across the desert.
For instance they know little about the details of the strike in town
and in the village, but it is enough that Mr Slime had spoken with
the shipping authorities and had made it clear they were not to
return till he had judged the conditions satisfactory.

The strike is led by the urban workers. They have greater social
and political awareness than the villagers—a phenomenon true
of most colonial revolts. But the agressive mood generated by the
strike infects the whole country.[1] In Creighton village, schools
are closed for the day; trade and work stops; there is expectation
in the air. We view the drama in town through the eyes of the
village. Again they don't quite understand what is happening;
rumours that fighting has broken out in the town add to their
fear. The taut atmosphere, confusion and fear is caught in

Lamming's short sentences, reporting as if he was both inside and outside the people's hearts:

> There was a kind of terror in the air. The villagers were quiet and frightened within. The sun came out and dispersed the rain clouds and soon it was bright all over the land. All the shops were closed. The school was closed. In the houses they tried to imagine what the fighting was like. They had never heard of anything like it before. They had known a village fight and they were used to fights between boys and girls. Sometimes after the cricket competition one village team for various reasons might threaten to fight with the opponent. These fights made sense, but the incidents in the city were simply beyond them. There was fighting in the city. That was all they were told, and they repeated the words and tried to guess who were fighting whom. But they couldn't follow it clearly. It wasn't Mr Forster or Bots' father or the overseer's brother who were fighting. It was simply the fighting. They were fighting in the city. And the fighting would spread in the village. That was all clear. And they couldn't say they understood that. (p. 193)

Gradually we learn what has happened in the city. A crowd of waterfront workers sent a delegation to the Governor. The sentries would not allow the delegation to pass. Hence fighting breaks out during which the police fire at the crowd and kill Po, a small boy. Rioting spreads in the town and into the surrounding villages. The peasants resent the town people, but watch with breathless expectation as the workers ambush Mr Creighton, who is saved from death by the timely arrival of Mr Slime. Disappointed, because they wanted to avenge Po's death, the men disperse. Soon the police arrive at the village with rifles and 'bayonets shining dull and deadly in the night' and things return to 'normal'.

Has anything happened? We are told, ironically, I think, that the years have changed nothing. The riots are not repeated, but things are clearly never the same again in the village. For the boy-hero, his immediate world has gradually withered away: 'where you wus sittin' wus a worl' all by itself, an' you got to get up an' go to the other world where the new something happen'. The break-up of the old is an inevitable process of growing up and what the boy uncomfortably feels—that he is seeing things for the last time—is part of the transition from adolescence to manhood. But his transition coincides with, or is a symbol of, a deeper historical experience the village community is about to undergo: the further dispossession of the peasants, thus adding them to the army of the rootless urban workers. This experience, as in many events in Lamming's novels, has a peculiar irony: the final dispossession logically follows their own agitation and their awakened consciousness. The strike and the riots make Creighton depart from the Estate; he sells the land to the Penny Bank and the Friendly Society. The people with the most shares get the first choice in the purchase of land and the house plots. These are lawyers, teachers, doctors and members of the legislative Assembly—in a word, the emergent national bourgeoisie.

> 'Tell me,' the shoemaker said (when given verbal notice to quit his home by the new owner) 'what sort o' nancy story you tell me 'bout you buy this lan'; how the bloody hell you can buy this, who sell it to you, where you get money to buy it from, since when you an' a white landlord is friends for him to call you in secret an' sell you a spot o' land that I been on for only God knows how long. This ol' shop been here for more'n twenty years, an' you come on a big bright morning like this to tell one some shitting story 'bout this spot belonging to you ...' (p. 246)

His incredulous outburst and protesting gestures are futile; he sobs loudly; he was one of the first and the most consistent followers of Mr Slime; he is painfully conscious of the irony that he, and the other peasants, had put 'signature' to a warrant for their exile. To emphasise that the process we are witnessing is the dispossession of the peasantry, the central importance of land is stressed over and over again.

> Houses were built and houses were sold in all parts of the island. But it was different with the land. This thing which stretched high and low and naked under the eye, the foot, the wind and the rain had always seemed to carry a secret buried somewhere beneath its black surface. Why did people respect land as they did? He didn't understand, but it was a kind of visitation that assisted or terrified, an infectious disease which money made imperative for the rich to inherit. The poor understood the same issue in a different way; since they couldn't own it, they rooted themselves into it. Dirt was cheap as the villagers often said, and sand was free; but land was the land, priceless, perennial and a symbol of some inexplicable power.

In this clash in which the peasants are exploited and dispossessed, turned into urban labourers even, we can hear echoes of a similar process in Africa and Latin America. The implacable power of money in this process and in destroying personal relationships is constantly emphasised. The feudal colonial relationship—Creighton's paternal 'responsibility' and the peasants' customary rights—is finished. Above all, cash now regulates personal relations inside the village. This is painfully brought home to us when the headmaster, a man who is respected in the village as the teacher of 'our' children and who is looked upon as a moral guide, buys the plot of land on which Pa has lived all his life. Pa is to go to an almshouse. He accepts this with stoic dignity but asks the teacher a series of puzzled questions: Why did Mr Creighton sell the land to the teacher? What was this strong relation between Mr Slime and the landlord? The headmaster cannot answer the questions. In fact few people involved in the break-up can explain what is happening because it can only be explained in a historical perspective and in terms of class struggle and solidarity. In the novel it is Trumper, who has been to America, who correctly sees the break-up in these terms. Because he has seen racial oppression and the struggle of Negro workers, Trumper discovers his solidarity with the oppressed back in the village; he speaks a different language, a language which not even the graduates of the secondary schools around can comprehend. Hearing that Pa is going to an almshouse, Trumper sums up the general pain current in the village:

'The Alms House,' said Trumper, ' 'Tis a place he would never ever go on his own accord in this life. He wus too decent, Pa. Slime couldn't look Pa in the face if it's a question o' dignity we talkin' 'bout. But that's life. 'Tis the way o' the world, an' in a world o' Slimes there ain't no way out for those who don't know how to be slimy.' (p. 294)

He advocates the united struggle of the dispossessed.

'You think they dare move all the houses?' he asked. 'If every one o' you refuse to pay a cent on that land, and if all o' you decide to sleep in the street let the government find room for you in the prison house, you think they dare go through with this business o' selling the land?' (p. 294)

He speaks in terms of exploitation:

'Way back he [Mr Slime] promise that he'd make these people here owners o' this land. He tell them there wasn't nothing to prevent them buying this lan' and he wus right, 'cause I know for a fact that the very money that go in the Penny Bank an' Society buy this land in his name. That's what I know. Nothin' he do ain't surprise me.'
     'There are others involved,' I said. 'I know some of them.'
     ' 'Course there is,' said Trumper. 'There's always more'n one in this kind o' deal ...' (p. 296)

Trumper brings a new level of thinking to bear on the situation in the village, in this way deepening their already awakened political consciousness. 'I am going to fight for the rights of negroes, and I'll die fighting,' he declares. Thus with the break-up of colonial feudalism we come to the edge of a new struggle of rootless peasants (now proletarianised, because exiled from the land) side by side with the urban workers against both the white colonial landlord and the emergent national bourgeoisie. The novel ends with a double exile: of the villagers from their plots, their home, their 'customary' land, their old relationships, and of G. from the village, going to Trinidad. But as in the case of Trumper, we are given hints that the moment of exile in urban industry in Trinidad, America, Britain, is also a moment of discovery of one's perspective in history and of identity of interests with one's people (or class).

In light of what has happened to the peasant masses in Africa, the West Indies, and all over the former colonial world, *In the Castle of My Skin* acquires symbolic dimensions and new prophetic importance: it is one of the great political novels in modern 'colonial' literature.

NOTE

1 The strike and social upheaval which make the central crisis in the novel and which are depicted as being part of the political consciousness in Barbados must obviously have been inspired by the series of labour and political troubles which swept across the British West Indies in the thirties. In St Kitt's sugar workers went on strike for more wages; in St Vincent, the Working Men's Association pressed for land reforms and a new constitution, while in Trinidad a mass of workers in the oil-fields rioted. The riots in Trinidad, for instance, are specifically mentioned in the novel. This period also saw the emergence of early nationalist and labour leaders like Bradshaw, Grantley Adams, Bustamante and Manley.

From 'George Lamming's *In the Castle of My Skin*', in *Homecoming* (London, Ibadan, Nairobi: Heinemann, 1972), pp. 110-26 (110-11, 114-26).

LLOYD W. BROWN

The Revolutionary Dream of Walcott's Makak

... The revolutionary 'dream' or the visionary quest of Walcott's Makak symbolically projects the psychological realities of the Black Man's relationship with both the White West and the African past. Makak (Felix Hobian), a charcoal vendor on a West Indian island, is jailed overnight for disorderly conduct. Strictly speaking, the play's action represents the fantasies which constitute Makak's dream-world and which are re-enacted in his mind during his overnight imprisonment; he is a Black Messiah whose quest for an African identity (he plans to return to Africa) is inspired by an 'Apparition' (an image of the White Woman). But Walcott does not allow us the luxury of viewing Makak's dream as an isolated, individual fantasy. For we are a part of his dream. And *our* implication is dramatised by the manner in which the 'spectators' *within* the play/dream are incorporated into Makak's visionary world; his cell-mates, Tigre and Souris, the jailor Corporal Lestrade, and Makak's partner, Moustique—they are all principal actors in Makak's 'fantasies' because, although they see him as a weak-headed old man, the dream also exists in *their* minds, and, implicitly, in the minds of the play's Black (theatre) audience.

In one sense, of course, our African dream and our revolutionary transcendentalism are a kind of escape. On its most elemental, sexual level, Makak's dream of a White goddess/apparition compensates for the fact that he is ugly ('macaque', the monkey), sexually repulsive, and lonely. And beyond this, the dream lifts him above the harshness of his everyday poverty; the vision of an African splendour compensates for the self-hate that is ingrained in the Black psyche in a White world. As Makak himself summarises, 'I have left death, failure, disappointment, despair in the wake of my dreams' (*Dream on Monkey Mountain*, New York, 1970 p. 305). But the nature of Makak's dream also touches upon the ambiguities and ironic self-conflicts of a Black revolutionary consciousness. For our revolutionary dreams are not merely a form of escape. They are also, paradoxically, a psycho-existential affirmation of self, of Black Selfhood. However overly idealistic his revolutionary cause may be, and despite the romanticisation of his 'royal' African Heritage, Makak affirms his human identity precisely because the capacity to dream has survived within him. Before his vision Makak is despised and self-hating, an impoverished hermit whose ugliness (that is, *Black* ugliness) makes Monkey Mountain an appropriate habitat (Monkeys are ugly, Black is ugly, and, of course, Blacks are monkeys/'makaks'). But at the end of his dream Makak expresses a triumphant sense of his own humanity which has been confirmed for us by his proven capacity for dreams. So that when he is released from prison the regaining of physical freedom is analogous to a birth, to revolutionary beginnings for Makak and his people:

> I have been washed from shore to shore, as a tree in the ocean. The branches of my fingers, the roots of my feet, could grip nothing, but now, God, they have found ground. Let me be swallowed up in mist again, and let me be forgotten, so that when the mist open, men can look up, at some small clearing with a hut, with a small signal of smoke, and say, 'Makak lives there. Makak lives where he has always lived, in the dream of his people.' Other men will come, other prophets will come, and they will be stoned, and mocked, and betrayed, but now this old hermit is going back home, back to the beginning, to the green beginning of this world. (p. 326)

In other words, the romantic fantasies about an African 'home' of royal lions act as a catalyst, enabling Makak and his people to come home to their human selves. The dream-fantasy about revolution involves and confirms a very real revolutionising of self-perception.

But this fantasy-reality paradox does not account for all the ambiguities which Walcott attributes to Makak's dream and its revolutionary ethos. For the very nature of Makak's vision emphasises a certain tension or self-conflict in the development of a revolutionary consciousness. Makak first hears the 'call' to a Black awareness from the 'Apparition' in his dream: 'She say I should not live so any more, here in the forest, frighten of people because I think I ugly. She say I come from the family of lions and kings' (p. 236). But the apparition is a White woman, the 'loveliest thing I see on this earth,/Like the moon walking along her own road' (p. 227). Makak's fascination with her White beauty is really the instinctive result of his self-hate as an old man who is 'ugly as sin'. He is a man

> Without child, without wife.
> People forget me like the mist on Monkey Mountain.
> Is thirty years now I have look in no mirror,

Not a pool of cold water, when I must drink,
I stir my hands first, to break up my image (p.226)

And her whiteness compensates for his self-hate as a Black man. In his own crude way Moustique who is really Makak's *alter ego* embodies this self-hate. Moustique's, and Makak's, ugliness and Blackness make the White woman (and, by extension, the white world) inaccessible—and therefore more desirable. According to Moustique's bitter reminder, 'You is nothing. You black, ugly, poor, so you worse than nothing. You like me. Small, ugly, with a foot like a "S". Man, together two of us is minus one.' (p. 237)

In effect, Makak's revolutionary consciousness is closely linked with the self-hate and whiteness of his pre-revolutionary phase. The revolutionising of his self-perception depends upon an intense awareness of the whiteness and self-hate; the Black man must recognise the latter for what they are—as integral parts of his own psyche—before he can deal with them. So that, initially, Makak's 'Black' pride, his reaching for some glorious African past of 'lions and kings', is an affirmation, rather than a negation, of his whiteness. For it is all aimed at proving some notion of humanity to the White world rather than to himself. And his revolutionary Black awareness can only be fully developed once he recognises that the Apparition represents his continuing and subconscious allegiance to the White world which his rhetoric rejects. Hence Corporal Lestrade, Makak's bourgeois *alter ego*, reminds him that he can only realise his total Black humanity by destroying an allegiance that saps his revolutionary potential:

What you beheld, my prince, was but an image of your longing. As inaccessible as snow, as fatal as leprosy. Nun, virgin, Venus, you must violate, humiliate, destroy her; otherwise, humility will infect you . . . She is lime, snow, marble, moonlight, lilies, cloud, foam and bleaching cream, the mother of civilisation, and the confounder of blackness. I too have longed for her. She is the colour of the law, religion, paper, art, and if you want peace, if you want to discover the beautiful depth of your blackness, nigger, chop off her head! When you do this, you will kill Venus, the Virgin, the Sleeping Beauty. She is the white light that paralysed your mind. (p. 319)

When Makak obeys, when he beheads the Apparition, the self-conflict ends, because in his words, he is now 'free'—free of White value systems and images which have stunted his Black self-awareness.

Altogether then, Makak's dream is a mirror which reflects the paradoxes in his emergent self-awareness. The full development of a Black revolutionary consciousness depends upon a frank recognition of the Whiteness within, and of the Black-White tensions which account for the Black man's notorious double-consciousness, but which, ironically, also spark his perceptual revolution by forcing him to confront his self-contradictions. And having recognised his self-hate and Whiteness for what it is, then he must destroy it before he can progress from his initial ambiguities (Black rhetoric, White Apparition) to the unequivocal freedom of Black self-acceptance. This is the kind of progression that the Black American critic Larry Neal describes; the Black revolution is an internal violence, 'the destruction of a weak spiritual self for a more perfect self. But it will be a necessary violence. It is the only thing that will destroy the double-consciousness—the tension that is in the souls of the black folk.' (*Black Fire*, ed. LeRoi Jones and Larry Neal, New York, 1969, p. 656.)

This, too, is the progression that is dramatised by the relationship between Makak and those who both inhabit and share his dream. Moustique, his coal-vending partner in real life, and Corporal Lestrade, the mulatto policeman who takes him in custody for the night, enter the dream as Makak's *alter egos*. And as such they join the Apparition herself to complete the contradictions of Makak's undeveloped Black consciousness. Moustique's ugliness is a physical reflection of Makak's self-loathing. Moreover, when Moustique turns Makak's popularity into a quick, monetary profit, he represents the exploitative motives that are inherent in the initial stages of Makak's revolutionary development. In the absence of a fully developed Black awareness, Moustique remains faithful to his racial self-loathing by using Makak's idealism as a means of exploiting a gullible and impoverished community. So that taken together, Makak and Moustique represent the ambiguity of the undeveloped revolutionary psyche. It combines the new revolutionary idealism with the exploitative instincts of the old self-loathing; and this destructive ambiguity can also be resolved when Moustique, like the Apparition, is purged from Makak's consciousness through a ritualistic execution.

By the same token, the extreme, anti-Black neuroses of the mulatto Lestrade re-enact Makak's self-hate. When Lestrade is 'converted' to Makak's Black cause, his rampaging militancy is a guilty reflex which seeks to compensate for the old bourgeois self-hatred. Hence, like Makak, Lestrade can only be truly free when he recognises the central paradox of the Black revolutionary consciousness—the psycho-existential link between the old self-hate and the new self-discovery. And he acknowledges this connection when he lectures Makak on the latter's need to destroy the Apparition ('I too have longed for her. She is the colour of the law, religion . . .'). In effect, Lestrade's earnest injunction to Makak is also a crucial confession of his own double consciousness. But, in symbolical terms, this is really Makak's confession, since Lestrade is his *alter ego*. Consequently, the Lestrade/Makak confession joins the execution of Moustique/Makak and the beheading of the Apparition; they are the initial purging which releases Makak into an untrammelled Black Selfhood. The revolutionary psyche which Makak's dream projects is now complete. He now returns to that other reality represented by the jail cell. But, as we have already seen, the very capacity to dream has confirmed his revolutionary possibilities ...

From 'Dreamers and Slaves: the Ethos of Revolution in Walcott and LeRoi Jones', *Caribbean Quarterly*, vol. 17 (September-December 1971), pp. 36-44 (37-41).

GORDON ROHLEHR

Blues and Rebellion: Edward Brathwaite's *Rights of Passage*

Coming to terms with the trilogy of Edward Brathwaite—*Rights of Passage* (1967), *Masks* (1968), and *Islands* (1969)—is indeed an immense task. Together these books are the monumental epic of a race, a kind of *Aeneid* or *Iliad* for Black people. Epic structure is employed only in *Masks*, which bears some affinity in theme, tone, and surprisingly enough in rhythm, to Anglo-Saxon elegiac poetry. In *Masks*, the wandering consciousness of the exiled African picks its painful way through the ruins, relics and lost cities of an identifiable but disastrous past. Yet the epic sense is there in *Rights of Passage*, where the archetypal themes of exile, journey, arrival and further journey, are sustained by a network of cross-references. In *Islands*, the exhausted nameless protagonist, a kind of Black Tiresias, returns home to the West Indies, and attempts to come to terms with the harsh paradoxes of life there. Arrival turns out to be a fresh departure into pain; a fresh journey into self. Home is where we start from.

More specifically, the trilogy reveals Brathwaite's concern as an Afro-West Indian who is both professional historian and poet, with coming to terms with his own history. There is the difficult matter of doing justice to a historiography which contains a high percentage of lies and crippling prejudice against the African, and to a history which makes intense emotional demands on the research student. Studying his history is often a traumatic and transfiguring experience for the Black man. He becomes possessed by the facts which he must shape into form, and justice becomes a personal, professional and *artistic* necessity. Brathwaite's research was clearly undertaken as what Gilberto Freyre calls an 'adventure in sensibility', which, in the opinion of Freyre, is what all serious study of history should be.[1] Brathwaite's research made a great deal of difference to his poetry, much of which had been appearing in West Indian journals like *Kyk-Over-Al*, *Bim*, and *Caribbean Quarterly* for some years. It gave it point and focus. It forced the poet into a tremendous quest for form to contain the fire with which he was now possessed.

The trilogy, though published in the last three years of the 1960s seems to have been in Brathwaite's head since the early 60s. Indeed, the 'Calypso' section of *Rights of Passage* had appeared in *Caribbean Quarterly* since 1956. At that time it took the form of a severe rejection of Anglo-Saxon tea-time tolerance towards Black students whom they could see only as visitors with white teeth from a land of sunshine and calypso. Brathwaite was attempting to destroy the stereotype. The poem 'Leopard' had appeared in *Bim* since 1961, while 'South' was published in *Caribbean Quarterly* in 1964. Also, a passage like 'Unrighteousness of Mammon' which is now in *Islands* was originally published in *Bim* in 1965 as part of *Rights of Passage*. In other words, far from being a sudden mushrooming of poetry, the trilogy can be seen as a gradual and sustained attempt by Brathwaite to come to terms with the spirit of West Indian history which has possessed him, and rides him as relentlessly as any Voudoun god. In his quest for form he is trying to be his own *houngan*, to control the resident *loa* and bring pattern to what can easily become wild uncontrolled movement.

In *Rights of Passage* Brathwaite has a look at the several faces, masks, poses and voices of the deracinated African in the New World. He is by turn Uncle Tom, Bigger Thomas, dilettante, 'gentleman or gigolo or both', politician, *arriviste*, humble villager or rebel. Each face has its voice and its music. Just as T. S. Eliot frequently used a musical image—Prelude, Rhapsody, Nocturne, Quartet—to describe his poetry, and claimed to be trying to discover the formal poetic equivalent to Beethoven's late quartets in his own *Four Quartets*, Brathwaite writes with reference to Black musicians such as Satchmo, Miles Davis, Charlie Parker, John Coltrane, the Jazzmen of Jamaica, and the chanting and drumming of Africanoid cults throughout the West Indies and in West Africa, where he lived for six years. He tries to achieve the verbal equivalent of the truths they first explored in their music; to shape a poetic form to match the forms each generation of Black musicians invented as it faced its own chaos.

Behind each movement of the long varied and uneven suite which is *Rights of Passage*, there is the poet's shifting consciousness, wandering like a Black Tiresias, understanding and fore-suffering all, and finally merging all the different voices into his own peculiar dry melancholy blues tone as he asks,

> Where *then* is the nigger's
> home?
> In Paris Brixton Kingston
> Rome?
> Or in Heaven?

Brathwaite himself in his notes to the Argo recording of his performance of *Rights of Passage* makes this point about the gradual fading out of all the different voices into that of a single consciousness. He writes:

> The *persona*, Tom, also undergoes a series of transformations—from ancestor to slave to prophet to Uncle Tom, and is finally translated into an image of the past out of which the future springs.

Rights of Passage begins with a Prelude, which, like a musical overture, states the themes that will be developed throughout the entire trilogy.

> Drum skin whip
> lash, master sun's
> cutting edge of
> heat, taut
> surfaces of things
> I sing
> I shout
> I groan
> I dream about
>
> Dust glass grit
> the pebbles of the desert:

The statement of theme here is bare, taut and skeletal, as if the bones of African experience were being uncovered. The movement of the verse is that of a slow painful journey over a wilderness of rock. The desert is both real and symbolic. It is the real desert which the migrating tribes crossed in their journey to the South of Sahara. This aspect of the African experience will be explored more fully in *Masks*. The desert is also the spiritual wilderness which the deracinated African continues to cross throughout history. This image of desert is connected with the theme of pestilence, blood-sucking flies, the worm, the rat gnawing at the roots of the sacred tree in *Masks*, and with the recurring images of whip, splintered glass, dust and sterility.

This original journey across the desert has become an archetypal tribal experience, which Brathwaite believes the later history of slavery, the middle passage and urbanisation, merely fulfills. Of this rootlessness Brathwaite writes:

> It is a spiritual inheritance from slavery and the long story before that of the migrant African moving from the lower Nile across the desert to the Western ocean, only to meet the Portuguese, and a history that was to mean the middle passage, America, and a rootless sojourn in the Caribbean sea. This

dichotomy expresses itself in the West Indian through a certain psychic tension, an excitability, a definite feeling of having no past, of not really belonging (which some prefer to call adaptability) and finds relief in laughter and (more seriously) in movement, dance, cricket, carnival, emigration.[2]

The trilogy is about all these things. Whether the poet is speaking of journey, exile, migration, dance, cricket, music, or worship, he is probing the same psyche. What this means is that the Afro-West Indian, behind all his roles and faces, possesses the possibility of a rich complex and integrated self, which is his by virtue of his exile—or, as Brathwaite puts it in *Islands*, 'by the holy ghost of his wounds'.

The narrator of the 'Work Song and Blues' section in *Rights of Passage* is Uncle Tom, 'father, founder, flounderer'. Tom has chosen life instead of defiant rebellion. It is his voice that establishes the muted melancholy of the Blues, which pervades the whole of *Rights of Passage*.

> Grow on, cotton
> lands
> go on to the bottom
> lands
> where the quick
> cassava grows
> where the sick
> back dries, where no one knows
> if he lives
> or dies.
> Blow on
> cotton blues.

Yet though this passage captures something of the desolation of the Blues, it misses the strength, rebellion and macabre laughter, the celebration of anarchy which earned the Blues the name of 'devil music'. This is inevitable since Uncle Tom disapproves of rebellion.

Yet, despite the fact that his children mock at his weak acquiescence, Tom is never really totally slave. Something in him refuses to accept the white man's legitimacy.

> Boss man makes rules;
> who works, who jerks
> the rope, who rips
> the patient dirt
>
> Boss man makes rules:
> I am his patient mule

> Boss man lacks pride
> so hides his
> fear of fear and darkness
> in the whip.

It is important to understand the complexity of Tom. His children never try. Capable of such perception, Tom is not altogether lost. Eldridge Cleaver made a similar point in his essay 'Allegory of the Black Eunuchs' where some young militants begin to understand and re-establish links with their fathers' generation. Cecil Taylor, a leading jazz pianist, declares:

> I didn't really understand my old man; well, you're from my generation and you know the difference between us and our fathers. Like, they had to be strong men to take what they took. But of course we didn't see it that way. So I feel now that I didn't really understand my father, who was really a lovely cat. He used to tell me to stay cool, not to get excited. He had a way of letting other people display their emotions while keeping control of his own.[3]

Uncle Tom may be an inhibiting influence on his children's psychic growth, but it is he who observes the histrionic quality of their rebellion; their uncertainty of self masked by over-loud speech and exhibitionist sexuality; their play-acting in front of the white man which can scarcely conceal the frenzy and confusion inside them.

> They call me
> Uncle Tom and mock me, . . .
> They laugh and the white
> man laughs: each
> wishing for mercy, each
> fearful of mercy, teach
> ing their children to hate
> their skin to its bitter root in the bone.

Tom, then, understands the degree to which his children have turned their rebellion inward, and anticipates that their self-mockery will continue for generations. His final wonder is whether his grandchildren will know a more gracious life beyond bitterness:

> Or do I hear them mock
> my sons: my own sons mock
> ing me?

The answer comes almost immediately in 'Folkways'. Here Tom's sons have drifted to the city, sing the railroad blues, become

spades, pimps and dilettantes, and suffer a further interment of the
self. The passage beginning 'I am a ... negro, man' has been
misinterpreted by some critics. Walcott complains that it is a
pathetically weak attempt to express the sort of rage that Césaire
and LeRoi Jones are good at. He is, however, identifying
Brathwaite too closely with the attitudes expressed by the narrator
at this stage. As Louis James observes, 'The statement is ironic: this
is how the whites see the negro, and the speaker explodes against
this.'[5] Yet this too is only partially correct, since the speaker
clearly believes some of the things he is saying. Thus, the irony may
be more the poet's than the speaker's. The real point, though, is
that whether the speaker believes what he is saying or not, he is
really caught in a situation which admits of little response except
an impotent rage:

> But get
> me out'a this place, you hear,
> where my dreams are wet as hell.

Next follows one of the most interesting experiments in the work.
Brathwaite mimetically reproduces, not with words alone, but with
sounds, the effects of a train journey. This little passage (p. 32),
which sounds very moving when well read, is more important than
first appears. Readers who are aware of the jazz context in which
the poem is being written, readily make the connection between this
passage and traditional railroad blues. The jazzmen of the twenties
and thirties took up the sounds of the railway horns and carriage
wheels, reproduced them on guitar, drums and brass, just as the
blues singers learned to imitate the cry of different trains. The
railroad blues with their strong sensation of travel, lie behind an
entire genre of jazz. What Brathwaite is doing here is establishing
the connection between Jazz and Journey; seeing jazz as yet
another gift of the archetypal experience in Africa, and its counter-
part in the New World. Today, every now and again, modern
jazzmen return to what they call the dirty blues, return to roots,
and celebrate afresh an exile and journey which has now become
traditional.

After this passage, there is a restatement of theme in 'The
Journeys'. It is a catalogue of the different journeys which the
African has been undertaking since the dawn of history. We begin
with Egypt, and as the journey widens out and we run through the
alphabet of exile, lines of verse lengthen to suggest this.

After this we are given a vision of the Black dilettante. Part
exploiter, part victim, he is ready to act out whatever role the
white world ascribes him, as long as it seems to be to his
profit.

> There
> he abides: himself, coursing his own
> man-
> oeuvres: jives calmly, merely nods
> his head and keeps
> his potent subterranean power
> for this his victim lover . . .

This is very fine irony indeed, the gift, no doubt, of Brathwaite's knowledge of what Billie Holiday was able to create out of a life of dismay. This constant 'man-oeuvring' is really a betrayal of both self and masculinity. Master of cadence, Brathwaite suggests in the half-blues, half-mocking be-bop diminuendo—surely a gift from Billie Holiday—that the Black gigolo-gentleman is surrendering self to the white death:

> taking
> his chance
> among the dead-
> ly follies with this
> nonchalance
> of shoulder and this
> urbane head.

The rest of *Rights of Passage*, with the brief exception of 'Calypso', 'South' and 'The Dust', is a sustained exploration of the predicament of the Black emigrant in any city:

> Castries, Conway and Brixton in London
> Port of Spain's jungle
> and Kingston's dry Dungle
> Chicago Smethwick and Tiger Bay.

In addition to this general picture of eternal tiredness and journey without arrival, Brathwaite looks at the political situation in the West Indies. His vision which tended at times to be blurred with nostalgia—as if failing rebellion the negro were capable only of a vague muted melancholy—becomes harder, sharper and more particular, thereby prefiguring *Islands*.

On the one hand, there is that fine portrait of the pathos and communion of village life, all the more impressive because Brathwaite, despite his debt to Lamming's *In the Castle of My Skin*, does not sentimentalise the lot of the peasant. 'The Dust' has been regarded by every critic as one of the major breakthroughs in the creative use of West Indian speech rhythms. Here the themes of pestilence and endurance, of humanity at the mercy of nature and the seasons, are explored, as the uneducated villagers come almost unconsciously to terms with existence itself.

In direct contrast to this world of the chattel house 'where beaten spirits/trapped in flesh/litter the landscape with their broken homes', is the world of the bourgeois *arriviste*, with its 'brilliant concrete crosses', padded cars, sticks of chrome-plated hire-purchase furniture, and

> soil-
> less, stain-
> less, name-
> less stalks
> of steel like New
> York, Paris,
> London town.

Again there is that exquisite sense of cadence. The emphasis on the '-less' in 'soil-less, stain-less, *name*-less' indicates the hygienic sterility, the lack of soul and roots in the privileged classes. They can only be defined in negative terms. Their world of inorganic steel—against which Césaire too raged—only seems solid, but the steel pylons are mere 'stalks' and can snap at any time. Also, the traditionally 'great' cities of the world, towards which the West Indian still orientates his life, are revealed for what they are, inhuman and too vast to know a single human cry. 'Police cars wail/like babies,/ . . . an elevator sighs/like Jews in Europe's gasses'. This is the world which Brathwaite sees the West Indies fast becoming—a world where machines have assumed human attributes, a nowhere land inhabited by nowhere people.

On the one hand, then, communion of village life threatened by the unexplained pestilence of the time, on the other, the *angst*, alienation and facelessness of arrivism, the final gift of the civilising West. In the midst of all this stride the politicians, stars of the show, with a supporting cast of a few million of the leaderless poor. The West Indian politician is most precisely and severely placed:

> each blind
> to that harsh light and vision that had once
> consumed them; eager now, ambitious,
> anxious that their single-
> minded fames should rise
> up uncorrupted from the foundry flames
> of time's unblemished brasses, while the
> supporting poor, famished upon their simple
> politics of fish and broken bread,
> begin to catch their royal asses . . .

The concentrated passion of these lines is but one of the many indices of the total disillusionment with Caribbean leadership which is running through West Indian societies. It is interesting that Brathwaite at this stage invokes the ghost of Uncle Tom, to show that it was an original failure to understand what he meant, a failure of empathy, which has led to this total acceptance of the soulless values of the new tourist-paradise societies. This point will be made finally late in *Islands*. Though at that stage the reader will be asked both to appreciate the full significance of Tom, and to negate his finally sterile conservatism and shame.

The inevitable result of all this frustration is the rebellion of Black youth, who either try to transcend misery by music, song and dance, to 'twist the music out of hunger' or bide their time in the dangerously calm pose of the Jamaican 'rudie boy', listening to his own blues, the Rock Steady.

> we winnin'
> we dinner
> is pick
> up we tools fuh the hit
> an' run raid
> an' you better
> look out for
> you wallet.
> An' watchin' me brother
> here sharpen 'e blade.

The final, ultimate result of this brutal life and history is that tragic, archetypal figure of Black rebellion, dignity and consciousness, the Rastafarian. Of all people in Jamaica, he alone is capable of defining his role in terms that seem to make some sense. Before looking at how Brathwaite presents the Rastafarian (whose voice returns in Negus's explosion of language in *Islands*), I would like to quote a Rastafarian on Rastafarianism:

I and I the Rastaman want the I-niversal world to hear what the Rastaman stand for. It is a first doctrine of the Rastaman, that the sick must nourish, the infant must care for, the aged must protect and the shelterless must shelter. So the true Rastaman don't have no spirit within himself that he would take even a material house built out of concrete nog or steel, until all suffering humanity—that is African in origin—that is scattered in all the West hemisphere, is taken off—until every human upon the face of creation stop live in paper hut, and live in dungeon, and go scuffle up on the dungle, and start off to get a better standard into a better government of God . . .

I would like to see the Government in Jamaica make some

preparation for the poor people that suffer malnutrition, sleep underneath swamps, and meet all kind of sickness and disease, and they die, and never see the face of the King of Kings and Lord of Lords.[6]

Here, then, is a people who are aware of their sacrificial role, who have assumed the priest-like burden of preserving the conscience of a society that has been accustomed to living without one. Interestingly enough, the artists in the society are aware of this, and the Rastafarian face pervades Jamaican art. As one who tries to come to terms with his fate, he immediately suggests himself to the artist as a symbol of strength and humanity. This is why he keeps appearing in the better Jamaican novels such as Roger Mais's *Brother Man* and *The Hills Were Joyful Together*, Orlando Patterson's *The Children of Sisyphus*, and John Hearne's *Land of the Living*.

In 'Wings of a Dove' Brathwaite tries to compress a great deal of his experience of Jamaica in small compass. Significantly, the Rastafarian is at its centre. It could scarcely be otherwise. The title of the poem is ironic. It derives from a Pocomania hymn which became a popular Ska tune in the early sixties. 'If I had the wings of a dove, I would like to fly away and be at rest'. Here, then, we have Uncle Tom's yearning for escape; the prayer for peace which is contained in the melancholy of Negro Spirituals. But the hymn continues: 'But I have no wings . . . ' There is therefore no escape. Brother Man knows this, and so he smokes in the only peace his milieu has to offer, the illegal pipe of ganja which alone can transform his poverty to riches, and make the mice eyes 'suddenly startle' like diamond.

The word 'startle' is well chosen, since it suggests the tension running beneath the surface of things, and the imminence of some sort of explosion. The detonation does take place in Brother Man's head.

> And I
> Rastafar—I
> . . .
> . . . rise and walk through the now silent
> streets of affliction, hawk's eyes
> hard with fear, with
> affection, and hear my people
> cry, my people
> shout:
>
> Down down
> white
> man, con

    man, brown
    man, down
    down full
    man, frown-
    ing fat
    man, that
    white black/man that/lives in/the town.

Brathwaite is able to bring us close to the bone of the Rastafarian experience, partly because he can create the drum rhythms of the cult. 'Wings of a Dove' is perhaps Brathwaite's most successful attempt in blending the rhythms of speech and music without doing much violence to either. So well does he do this that here *rhythm becomes image*, and contributes integrally to the 'meaning' of the poem. The world of the Rastafarian is also the world of the Ska, a militant work-song-type beat which Jamaica's deprived classes created in the late 1950s. Ska bears some affinity to Be Bop, both in the rebellion implicit in its energy, and because a number of popular musicians in Jamaica took a deep interest in jazz, and successfully translated what they derived rom the American Black musician, into the local idiom.

'Wings of a Dove' transports the reader back to the world of Roger Mais; of Ras Daniel Heartman, that formidable Rastafarian artist who brings out the strength and pride of Black faces better than anyone I know; of Don Drummond, that mighty trombonist of the sixties, whose music contained all the loneliness, doom and rebellion which are part of the Rastafarian experience.[7] It is an entire milieu that Brathwaite has recreated, through the marriage of language and music.

By trying to explore the total self of the Rastafarian, Brathwaite has completely destroyed the stereotype figure that the rest of society has trained itself to see. Brother Man, who owes something to Roger Mais's hero, is not the white man's bad nigger or the brown man's scapegoat. Indeed, he can see the privileged 'clean-faced' members of his society as vultures without any real roots. Brother Man is a representative figure because of the force with which he seeks to affirm what he is and remain who he is. Unlike the speaker in 'Folkways', Brother Man acts a role for no one. Caught in the tragic necessity for violent rebellion, he hugs his identity to him with force, love, and a kind of despair—despair, because Brother Man can only dream of Apocalypse. His vision of wings soaring high over the earth, is a dream, induced by the same opium that turned the eyes of the destroying mice to rubies and diamonds. At the end of his walk through 'the now silent streets of affliction', his dream of the destruction of Babylon is no nearer fulfilment. In *Islands*, the barrier between dream and reality is much thinner. Rebellion there is a caged leopard, ready to spring, waiting only for someone to open the cage door.

In the light of all this, the Epilogue, which begins by restating the 'Drumskin whip lash theme' but develops into a hopeful declaration:

> . . . scorched
> hurts continue
> to glow
> but my people know
> that the hot
> day will be over
> soon . . .

and an affirmed hope that just as the Ark eventually touched green land, Noah's pariah grandchildren, the Blacks, will soon shatter their barrier and walk in the morning, seems rather like the Rastafarian's dream, a simultaneous blend of hope and despair . . .

From 'Islands', *Caribbean Studies*, X (January 1971), pp. 173-202 (173-83).

NOTES

1 Freyre, G. *The Masters and the Slaves* (New York: Knopf, 1946), p. xxxvii.
2 Brathwaite, L. E. 'Roots', *Bim*, vol. X, no. 37 (July-December 1963), p. 10.
3 Spellman, A. B. *Four Lives in the Be-Bop Business*, (New York, 1966), p. 50.
4 Walcott, D. 'Tribal Flutes', *Sunday Guardian* (Trinidad), 19 March 1967.
5 James, L. Review of *Rights of Passage, Caribbean Quarterly*, vol. XIII, no. 1 (March 1967), p. 39.
6 Heymans P. (ed.), 'What the Rastaman Sey', *Public Opinion* (Jamaica), 12 June 1964, p. 8.
7 Rohlehr, G. 'Sounds and Pressure: Jamaica Blues', *Moko* (Trinidad), nos 16 and 17, 6 and 20 June 1969. See also G. White, 'Rudie Oh Rudie', *Caribbean Quarterly*, vol. 13, no. 3 (September 1967), and J. Carnegie, 'Notes on the History of Jazz and its Role in Jamaica'. *Jamaica Journal*, vol. IV, no. 1 (March 1970), pp. 20-9.

V.S. Naipaul and the New Order:
A View of *The Mimic Men*

V. S. Naipaul's fiction describes the fortunes of an emergent country. His novels can be said to define the transition from colonialism to independence. The emergent country is based on Trinidad, where he grew up, and it is generally identified as such, but the same thing 'has happened in twenty countries'. Despite all this, despite his services as a chronicler, or connoisseur, of political change, his subject matter can often seem like a kind of pre-politics. He is certainly far from enthusiastic about the kind of politics that enfranchisements and elections have accustomed us to.

Naipaul is not an *avant-garde* writer, and he has not received the indulgence, and the long, inspecting essays, that *avant-garde* writers frequently attract. There could be no cult of Naipaul. He favours picaresque narratives or swift comic treatments. But, if his books are not difficult, they are not simple either. Here, for example, is someone with conservative leanings who nonetheless writes movingly about the poor and aspiring, a compassionate man who is also fastidious and severe. To regard him as one of those Commonwealth writers who specialise in local colour and stories of exploitation is therefore a mistake. He is very possibly the best of the younger British novelists, and his translation from the Caribbean to the metropolis is among the posthumous benefits conferred by the old principle of Imperial Preference.

His early books were a little deceptive, admittedly, by virtue of their approximation to the 'Commonwealth literature' stereotype. They provide local colour, both sorts of colour; they even have, I suppose, childlike natives. A distinctive elegance was evident from the start, however, and it becomes clear in retrospect that the themes of the embellished early books are closely related to those developed in the later and weightier ones. The emergent country had started to emerge.

... *The Mimic Men* ... directly portrays the new order and completes the model of an emergent country. It is possible to doubt the credibility of *The Mimic Men*, but there can be no doubt that Naipaul's account of colonial freedom in the West Indies depends

to a great degree on the contrast between that novel and *Mr Biswas*.
Something of the significance of this contrast is conveyed by a
dictum from *The Mimic Men:* 'hate oppression; fear the oppressed'.
Whereas Mr Biswas is one of the oppressed, Ralph Singh is not.
A thriving real estate man, he becomes a nationalist leader. Mr
Biswas is compelled at one point to consider the 'immemorially
low' profession of barber, while for Ralph Singh 'the lowly barber'
is almost past pity: 'How can this man endure? How, running his
hands daily through the hair of other people, can he bear to keep
on?' Mr Biswas is condescendingly treated by the celebrity whom
he interviews for his newspaper. Singh studies the journalist who
interviews him 'with the eye of pure compassion'. The journalist's
'shining tie, his young face fussy and tired with worry, his
uncertain voice attempting bluntness', might be those of Mr Biswas
in his role as overwrought reporter. Despite the differences between
them, however, both Biswas and Singh are rebels. For Mr Biswas,
the old order had a matriarchal aspect, and for Singh this is also
the case—his mother's family have much of the authority of the
Tulsis. At the outset, he is drawn to their shiftless, privileged
existence, but also to the clever boys, of all ranks and races, at
his grammar school. In both books, a humiliated father turns into
a dissenter. Singh joins his father in dissent, though his father
belongs to the old order rather than the new: 'he fitted into the
pattern of dependence'.

The Mimic Men is told in a complicated fashion, with flashbacks
that give rise to a certain amount of mechanical trouble. Some
scenes are set in England, where Ralph lives as a student and
marries Sandra from North London—an acute portrait. They
return together to Isabella, but in due course they separate. His
notorious, absent father furnishes a means of entry into politics,
and as an ally of ·the oratorical Negro Browne he is elected to
power. Power, though, proves a mirage, and his popularity
crumbles—as did that of Ganesh—at a time of labour unrest. He
retires to a contemplative life in a London suburban hotel: a
Sabine-seeming retreat very suitable for someone who, when the
political crucible was at its hottest, had been in the habit of reading
Latin literature and annotating the campaigns of Pompey. His
experience of power—as a traveller in ministerial cars and the
companion of enlightened sugar magnates—is over.

The Mimic Men poses the well-known problem of 'point of view':
how far, that is, is the first-person narrative an attempt to charac-
terise a particular politician and how far is it designed to express
the writer's own sentiments? The problem will not appear very
formidable to certain of his readers in the Caribbean, who will be
inclined to treat the novel as Naipaul's political testament, and to
scan it for traces of disaffection, for racist or reactionary

tendencies. These readers may well call attention to the various resemblances between the opinions of Ralph Singh and the opinions set down in *The Middle Passage*. The resemblances can't be ignored; but I feel that the author has to be distinguished from his fairly supercilious hero, a narcissist and dandy who can refer to people as 'churls' and who dreams of retiring to one of those beautiful old estate houses—there are few left—on 'one of our former slave plantations' (a distancing touch, that, surely). As a counterweight to *The Middle Passage, Mr Biswas* encourages one to make the distinction between the author and his hero: *Biswas* is not a polemical work, but it 'hates oppression' and lends no ear to Singh's injunction about 'fearing the oppressed'. The whole of Naipaul's writing, the total testament, has to be brought into the picture. Even then, however, the problem, in respect of this particular novel, persists, and is at its least tractable on issues to do with emergent politics. On these issues Ralph Singh, from his Sabine standpoint, has a good deal to say.

Order and destruction, corruption and truth—the novel harks back to such ideas continually. Life in Isabella, as evoked by the narrator, can sometimes seem immemorially low. It is a 'tainted island' (the London suburbs are 'tainted' too, but only with traffic). 'We lack order', the new politician discovers; and it turns out later that Isabella has always lacked order. 'To be born on an island like Isabella, an obscure New World plantation, second-hand and barbarous, was to be born to disorder.' Singh's genera-tion are the 'mimic men of the New World, one unknown corner of it, with all its reminders of the corruption that came so quickly to the new'. These reflections, together with Singh's adolescent dream of riding across plains under snow-capped peaks (a Hindu's contemplation of Aryan power and spaciousness), suggest a perspective of antiquity against which Isabella's jumble of quarrel-some, recently arrived communities can hardly seem imposing. That Aryan dream, incidentally, makes an interesting contrast with the touching song which Mr Biswas, an altogether humbler Indo-European, used to croon on his Slumberking mattress: 'In the snowy and the blowy ...'

Once, Isabella was a 'colony, a benevolently administered dependency'. Now, after the interregnum of small-town grafting politicians who fitted into the old pattern of dependence, a generation of enthusiastic, demagogic, nationalistic politicians has taken power, only to find it an illusion, to find themselves afraid. 'I write', Singh explains, 'from both sides.' He speaks for the old and the new orders alike:

I cannot do otherwise. My mother's father was no doubt an undignified figure, an object of easy satire. But at least at the end, within the framework of our old order, benevolence and service were imposed on him. And he was never as totally ridiculous as the men we put in his place: men without talent or achievement save the reputed one of controlling certain sections of the population, unproductive, uncreative men who pushed themselves into prominence by an excess of that bitterness which every untalented clerk secretes. Their bitterness responded to our appeal. And in this response we saw the success of our appeal, and its truth!

Whatever Singh may claim, this passage says more for one side than for the other, and so—without being rancorous or 'satirical'—does the novel as a whole. But the praise given to authority and dependency, and the acid view of democracy, are nowhere attended by any clear or sustained impression of the colonial past. And quite enough is known about that past for Naipaul's use of words like 'benevolence' to seem tendentious to many.

This is likely to be a reason why the novel can at times appear incoherent and problematical:

I had never thought of obedience as a problem. Now it seemed to me the miracle of society. Given our situation, anarchy was endless, unless we acted right away. But on power and the consolidation of passing power we wasted our energies, until the bigger truth came: that in a society like ours, fragmented, inorganic, no link between man and the landscape, a society not held together by common interests, there was no true internal source of power, and that no power was real which did not come from the outside. Such was the controlled chaos we had, with such enthusiasm, brought upon ourselves.

Here, the new politician learns the lesson that small, recent, multiracial societies don't work (though you could be forgiven for thinking that Miguel Street worked, and wasn't all that fragmented and inorganic). Such passages might very well earn the retort that the stress on 'true' and 'real' is excessive, that there just isn't that much difference between one society and another. And on this particular occasion the narrator himself questions whether the lesson he has learned may not 'perhaps' be 'the vision of hysteria'. 'Like Browne,' he remarks, 'I was no politician.' Yet, in a puzzling way, the lesson is allowed to stand: one of the 'truths' of emergent politics is that they are a charade. Browne and Singh walk to the platform like actors in a play:

Add the smell of Negro sweat as, to applause, we make our way through our followers, shining eyes in shining faces, to the platform, they so squat and powerfully built, we so tall and slender. In this smell of heated sweat, once rejected, I tried to find virtue, the virtue of the poor, the labouring, the oppressed. Such is the vulgarity that mobs generate, in themselves and in their manipulators. The virtue I found in that acrid smell was the virtue of the protecting, the massed and heedless. It was Browne's privilege to be less sentimental. 'The old *bouquet d'Afrique,*' he would mutter. And sometimes, when we were on the platform: 'Did you get the old booky?'

Singh's claim that he is no politician is a reminder that Naipaul is no politician, either. In this, his most political novel, he is none-theless interested in private rather than public lives, just as in general he is interested in matriarchy for its own sake as well as for its capacity as metaphor to bring to mind other forms of dominion. But the novel is also about political action, even though the politics is the least impressive part of it, and I don't believe that this pair of leaders is offered as wholly idiosyncratic, or atypical. They can hardly be that if the same thing 'has happened in twenty countries': politics throughout the world has a way of recruiting those who are 'no politicians'. And, if the novel is about political action, then the sense of politics communicated by the narrator lives up to his own description: it is apt to seem obscurely visionary, and a little hysterical. How far, though, does the novelist mean us to think so? What is his point of view?

Perhaps the most important consideration is this: if Naipaul dissociates himself from his character, there is no way of being sure how far he dissociates himself. In the end, we must go by what is mostly there, by what the book will be read for. It will be read in the West Indies and in the world at large for the feelings by which it is governed. It will not be read for its disclaimers and its cautionary touches.

Those who are not acquainted with Trinidad will be reluctant to judge Naipaul's successive pictures of graft and futile enthusiasm. On the other hand, Isabella is presented as a typical new country and it is worth comparing it with the known histories of certain of the others. Naipaul has visited and written about Guyana (formerly British Guiana), and I am convinced that his experience of it helped him to write this novel. He reports in *The Middle Passage* that

a positive nationalism existed in British Guiana in 1953. This was the achievement of the Jagans and Mr Burnham and their colleagues, and it was destroyed by the suspension of the constitution in that year and—gratuitous humiliation—by the dispatch of troops. Colonial attitudes, so recently overcome, easily reasserted themselves.

Since *The Middle Passage* and *The Mimic Men* were written, information has come to light which suggests that ten years later the British and American governments, and the CIA, were actually concerned to engineer a reversion to colonial rule. This may perhaps be taken to illustrate the truth contained in *The Mimic Men* that 'no power was real which did not come from the outside'. But the novel has nothing comparable to the Jagans' 'positive nationalism' or to their private virtues as disclosed by Naipaul in his travel book: he stayed with them, watched them electioneering, and lunched in the country with Cheddi Jagan's mother. In my view, and in Naipaul's, the Jagans are serious and upright politicians; there is nothing mimic about them. Their troubles were not a matter of a theatrical chaos of powerlessness, but of difficult social problems compounded by conventional political challenges and subversions such as other countries elsewhere in the world have had to face. Whether or not their troubles resulted from the inherent defects and contradictions of an inorganic community, they also required neo-colonial intervention and the frown of Mr Dean Rusk.

The Mimic Men does not really do justice to the intricate difficulties inherited by those in the Jagans' position, to the causes of those upheavals which the new states inevitably undergo. Colonial rule is not the ideal preparation for a comfortable independence. Charitable as Naipaul is to his new politicians, he is not charitable enough, and it is worth comparing his 'man of the people'—as Browne is referred to—with the Nigerian politicians described in Chinua Achebe's *A Man of the People*, Achebe and Naipaul being unquestionably the most accomplished of the emergent novelists.

A man who has just come in from the rain and dried his body and put on dry clothes is more reluctant to go out again than another who has been indoors all the time. The trouble with our new nation—as I saw it then lying on that bed—was that none of us had been indoors long enough to be able to say 'To hell with it'. We had all been in the rain together until yesterday. Then a handful of us—the smart and the lucky and hardly ever the best—had scrambled for the one shelter our former rulers left, and had taken it over and barricaded themselves in. And from within they sought to persuade the rest through numerous loudspeakers, that the first phase of the struggle had been won and that the next phase—the extension of our house—was even more important and called for new and original tactics; it required that all argument should cease and the whole people speak with one voice and that any more dissent and argument outside the door of the shelter would subvert and bring down the whole house.

This is very moving; it is also both realistic and humane. Everywhere in the world, emergent can turn into insurgent, and Nigeria is now in tumult; there have been chicaneries and murders; the Eastern Region has seceded (and Achebe along with it). But it need not be assumed that this is the end of the world for the societies of Nigeria, or for its dissenters. It can be said of *The Mimic Men* that it does not hold out much hope for its area of darkness; the end of that world is felt to be near. Not every one of its readers, however, will be persuaded that this is the case.

The occasional obscurities of *The Mimic Men* may in part be due to the novelist's long absence from the West Indies. It is the fate of Commonwealth writers to find out that their most fertile subject matter lies in their native country, and that when they leave they run the risk of losing it. Trying for new subjects, or, alternatively, keeping up the old ones and so, in effect, establishing a recourse to the past and working with material which is very hard to replenish, can be torture. Naipaul, who has tried both of these alternatives, chose a new subject in *Mr Stone and the Knights Companion*, which preceded *The Mimic Men*. This is a comedy of manners about South London: the writer takes pleasure in the deals and treasons of Mr Stone's circle, and makes it a sort of sooty, strangulated, boring Miguel Street, with its own fragmented, none-too-organic community life. Mr Stone is like Pooter. He is a nobody: not just humble and got down like Mr Biswas, but without his wit or stumbling pertinacity, as of a man clowning his way on a tightrope across the classic yawning gulf. Mr Stone's only charm is to possess a certain infinitely embarrassed decency, and, ironically enough, it is this decency which enables him at last, for he is more or less pensionable, to shine in the huge firm where he works. It is presided over by another of Naipaul's liberal magnates, who is sympathetic to Mr Stone's amorphous scheme whereby retired employees of the firm are to attend and assist each other in the evening of their days. Stone's thunder, though, is stolen by the public relations colleague who is appointed to get the scheme off the ground and who dubs their pensioners the Knights Companion.

In this novel, Naipaul renounces his multi-racial characters and colonial themes. To write about the English—the domestic English, moreover, at their sootiest and drabbest—is something which no West Indian novelist would lightly undertake. In fact, it is the lightness of the novel which assures its success. The ironic elegance of the early work reappears. Half-baked, stately Mr Stone is a study in eccentricity of a kind which belongs naturally to a comedy of manners. And that is the point. His eccentricities are proper to a comedy of manners and are no more marked or exaggerated than are those of the worthies of Miguel Street. They are not there as a means of dissembling the blankness or condescension of the unacclimatised observer. Besides being Indian and Trinidadian, Naipaul is also English.

Naipaul has eccentricities of his own. You feel that he is prejudiced, that his quirkiness is intense. A patrician austerity, for example, and a cruel or punitive refinement which is fully attested by the haughty, lingering encounters with whores and foreign students in *The Mimic Men*, are addressed to descriptions of crudity and deprivation; yet, there is no hint of condescension or paternalism. Such idiosyncrasies, however, are reassuring as well as alarming. As with a number of august predecessors—and Lawrence might be named as one—they can even be regarded as the ground of his achievement, an earnest of the fidelities afforded by his work. They register as signs of suffering; at the same time they can very nearly persuade you that only someone so prejudiced could be so fair. This might look like a rather grim and gnomic paradox (which enforces sharp distinctions within the body of the work in question). But there is a passage in Naipaul about the West Indian writer, and about the desirability of malice, which may help to explain it:

It is not easy to write about the West Indian middle class. The most exquisite gifts of irony and perhaps malice would be required to keep the characters from slipping into an unremark-able mid-Atlantic whiteness. They would have to be treated as real people with real problems and responsibilities and affec-tions—and this has been done—but they would also have to be treated as people whose lives have been corrupted by a fantasy which is their cross. Whether an honest exploration of this class will ever be attempted is doubtful. The gifts required, of subtlety and brutality, can grow only out of a mature literature; and there can be advance towards this only when writers cease to think about letting down their sides.

In his own fiction, subtlety and brutality co-exist and are somehow inseparable, just as, at other levels, cruelty and crudity, purity and poverty, also co-exist, at times bewilderingly. He is in favour of 'a little blow every now and then'. What makes the brutality bearable, and desirable, is precisely that it seems to be that of a real and suffering person, 'with real problems and responsibilities and affections', and has nothing of the partisan about it. He does not care about letting down the side. Indeed, it can be said of him, as Singh said of himself, that he 'writes from both sides,—an impart-iality which is only impaired by a tenderness for (in Caribbean contexts) Asian things. He is the very opposite of the kind of 'liberal' novelist who is widely, and with reason, distrusted now;

and this may well have excited suspicions among the West Indian Left that he is a bit of a Fascist, bearing a cross of Aryan fantasies. These suspicions are only to be expected. Malice provokes reprisals; 'subtlety and brutality' lay themselves open to misrepresentation. At all events, he has achieved a mature literature.

From 'V. S. Naipaul and the New Order', *Kenyon Review*, vol. 29 (November 1967), pp. 685-98 (685-6, 690-8).

PART III

Relationships: Individual, Community, Mankind

DAVID ORMEROD

'Unaccommodated Man': Naipaul's B. Wordsworth and Biswas

... In the childlike story of the life and death of the failed poet
B. Wordsworth, Naipaul constructs an image which the reader
might well take as emblematic of both Naipaul's own predicament
as a West Indian novelist and the predicament of Biswas. The
narrator, as a boy, meets the itinerant Negro poet B. (for Black)
Wordsworth, who tells the boy that he is engaged on the composition of the greatest poem in the world, to which he adds one line
a month, in the hope that this one line will be the distillation of a
whole month's experience. We are only told one line—the bathetic,
'The past is deep'. Dying, the poet says that the poem is not going
well: the poem that he asserts he is composing is in fact his own
life. He also tells the boy, elliptically, the reason for his isolation
and loneliness—a story of a dead wife and a still-born child. Yet,
on his death bed, he denies the validity of the two myths by which
he has cherished his life; there is no poem, and there was no girl-
wife. Returning to the poet's cottage a year later, the boy finds that
it has disappeared and has been replaced by an office block.

The story is in many ways trite and sentimental, yet the paradoxes of Black Wordsworth's life give us an epitome of the
predicament of the artist in a colonial society. Black Wordsworth
tries to live the patterns established for him by his brother W.
(White) Wordsworth; he contemplates bees and flowers, takes
refuge in the role of aesthetic recluse. The past is a burden which
cripples him. He tries to deny its power, and the few words he
produces are clichés. His function is simply to exist, to embody
in however inadequate a way the creative drive in a society which
provides no outlet for creativity. This short story, with the lonely
figure of B. Wordsworth at its centre, is Naipaul's first tentative
draft of an image which is later to become an obsession with him.
Miguel Street was the third of Naipaul's works to be published,
but the first to be written (*v.* Naipaul's interview with David Bates,
Sunday Times, London, 26 May 1963), and in B. Wordsworth, with
his undirected aesthetic leanings and frustrated creativity, we can
see the progenitor of Ganesh Ramsumair of *The Mystic Masseur*
(London, 1957), stranded in the hot and dusty village of Fuente

Grove, surrounded by books (mostly unread) which he values for
their footage, starting innumerable notebooks and never finishing
them. In Naipaul's travel book, *The Middle Passage* (London,
1962), this 'derelict man in a derelict land' (p. 190) becomes an
almost explicit embodiment of the West Indian experience, when
Naipaul relates his encounter with such a man in Surinam, seeing
in him the image of a society whose members are abducted from
Africa or duped into quitting India, only to be abandoned in the
alien colonial wilderness. Hence, 'The past is deep', for 'nothing
was created in the British West Indies, no civilisation as in Spanish
America, no great revolution as in Haiti or the American colonies
. . . . The history of the islands can never be satisfactorily told.
Brutality is not the only difficulty. History is built around achievement and creation; and nothing was created in the West Indies'
(*The Middle Passage*, p. 29). The pin which B. Wordsworth tells
the boy to drop into the harbour sinks immediately, despite the
poet's assurance that we live in a strange world, just as all Mr
Biswas' attempts to find romance in the sterile society that surrounds him seem to founder. Returning to the house of the dead
poet, the boy finds that his beloved trees have been cut down, 'and
there was brick and concrete everywhere. It was as if B. Wordsworth
had never existed' (p. 65), just as Mr Biswas returns to the village
where he was born to find that it has disappeared, for the land was
rich in oil and is now a garden suburb: 'The world carried no
witness to Mr Biswas' birth and early years' (p. 38). The world
contemptuously denies all the individual's attempts to assert his
dignity and difference, and Naipaul's major novel narrates the
attempts of an individual to fight back against this cosmic denial
of his very existence. How dreadful, then, 'to have lived without
even attempting to lay claim to one's portion of the earth; to have
lived and died as one had been born, unnecessary and unaccommodated' (p. 13). Naipaul himself is evidently very conscious of
the importance of this theme in his work. In the interview with
David Bates, cited earlier, he says that the main literary influence
exerted on him so far has been that of his father, for 'other writers
are aware that they are writing about rooted societies; his work
showed me that one could write about another kind of society'—
the rootless, impermanent world whose flux and mutability Mr
Biswas tries to defy. Or, as another critic remarks, 'The book is
about Mohun Biswas' will to make a dent in the world, to leave
behind him something of value—in his case, a house. It is also
about his effort and struggle to give his own life some shape and
purpose and meaning, in a situation which, from the first, renders
him almost powerless to do so.'[1]

It is perhaps significant that the crisis of the breakdown is
prompted by an unusual moment of insight on Biswas' part, an

insight not only into his own situation but into the whole West Indian predicament—the predicament of a nomadic society, a wanderer in space and time, which can find no anchorage. It is often the predicament of the artist, but seems necessarily the predicament of the frustrated West Indian artist, whether he is B. Wordsworth, producing one passionate platitude a month, or Mr Biswas, who worked 'more and more elaborate messages of comfort for his walls with a steady, unthinking hand, and a mind in turmoil' (p. 259). Biswas now sees the significance of his own nomadic life, for he feels that for too long he has regarded each stage in his life as temporary. He therefore decides not to plan for any hypothetical future, but to savour the richness of each passing action. He deliberately starts to read and relish a novel, but his mental image of himself as a civilised man inhabiting a clearing in the jungle of the world's barbarity shifts to the image of a man trapped in a billowing black cloud, the void into which he at last tumbles. It seems to him, suddenly and too late, that all his life has been happy, but that he has always denied his own content-ment, so that now he is swamped by 'grief for a happy life never enjoyed and now lost . . . He forced himself to cry for all his lost happiness' (pp. 241-2).

And so, the crisis comes with the violence of the storm which blows down the ramshackle frame of the abortive house, and Biswas, like Lear, chooses to quit the safety of the labour lines and sit in the windswept wreckage until, like Lear again, he becomes the basic 'unaccommodated man' whom Naipaul describes in the Prologue—'unnecessary and unaccommodated'. During the storm myriads of ants appear and Anand tries to massacre them, but they mount his stick and bite his arm. 'He was suddenly terrified of them, their anger, their vindictiveness, their number' (p. 262), as if they stood for the teeming masses of Hanuman House who cannot be defied. And, indeed, the little creatures seem to exult in Biswas' destruction with as great a relish as do the Tulsis: '. . . the rain and wind swept through the room with unnecessary strength and forced open the door of the drawing room, wall-less, floor-less, of the house Mr Biswas had built . . . lightning flashed intermittently, steel blue exploding into white, showed the ants continually disarranged, continually reforming' (p. 263)'.

His recuperation at Hanuman House is a period when the entire environment, of The Chase, Green Vale, the whole of the Trinidad ethos, can be mercifully held in suspense, for 'surrender had removed the world of damp walls and papercovered walls, of hot sun and driving rain, and had brought him this: this wordless room, this nothingness' (p. 269). Curled like a foetus in the darkness, he awaits a rebirth, a rebirth to new life, from the countryside and communalism of the first part of the novel to the town and individualism of the second, an environment in which the old Hanuman House organism gradually breaks up, leaving only individuals. The last sentence of the first half harks back to the title of the first chapter—'Pastoral'—and the whitewashed palm trees outside Hanuman House are like the mudcaked legs of Pratap and Prasad as boys, fresh from the buffalo pond. A grim pastoral, for the lush elegance of Arcadia is far from the sunbaked mud of Trinidad.

. . . One of the devices by which the individualism and tenderness of B. Wordsworth's personality is fixed in the reader's attention involves the luxuriant foliage of his garden. He first acquires the boy's companionship by promising him fruit from his garden, a garden whose vegetation sets the poet apart from the undifferentiated city dwellers. 'The yard seemed all green. There was the big mango tree. There was a coconut tree and there was a palm tree. The place looked wild, as though it wasn't in the city at all. You couldn't see all the big concrete houses in the street' (p. 59). The trees embody the life that burgeons in the poet, and when the boy returns to the house a year later, the poet's destruction is paralleled by the fate of his trees—'The mango tree and the plum tree and the coconut tree had all been cut down, and there was brick and concrete everywhere. It was as though B. Wordsworth had never existed' (p. 65). The poet has failed to leave a mark of his presence in the world, just as Biswas would have failed but for the final acquisition of the house. As Biswas' life is a story of the battle against his hostile environment, so the changes in his fortunes are marked by the state of the vegetation which surrounds him. At Green Vale, for instance, the environment is symbolic (p. 185):

> Whenever afterwards Mr Biswas thought of Green Vale he thought of the trees. They were tall and straight, and so hung with long, drooping leaves that their trunks were hidden and appeared to be branchless. Half the leaves were dead; the others, at the top, were a dead green. It was as if all the trees had, at the same moment, been blighted in luxuriance, and death was spreading at the same pace from all the roots. But death was forever held in check. The tongue-like leaves of dark green turned slowly to the brightest yellow, became brown and thin as if scorched, curled downwards, over the other dead leaves, and did not fall. And the new leaves came, as sharp as daggers; but there was no freshness to them; they came into the world old, without a shine, and only grew longer before they too died.

Here, evidently, is a comment on Biswas' life; the death-in-life appearance of the trees is a parallel to his own existence, and as the leaves came into the world old, so did Biswas, who bore the title 'Mr' even as a new-born child—'Some time later they were awakened by the screams of Mr Biswas' (p. 15). The new leaves without a shine recall the scrofulous infant, Biswas, 'dusty and muddy and unwashed . . . with eczema and sores that swelled and burst and scabbed and burst again . . .' (p. 21). Images of blighted growth and desiccated vegetation also mark the period of the stay in the Tulsi house in Port of Spain; the rose trees Biswas attempts to tend, like the trees at Green Vale, mirror his condition: 'A blight made their stems white, and gave them sickly, ill-formed leaves. The buds opened slowly to reveal blanched, tattered blooms covered with minute insects . . .' (p. 340), the insects perhaps standing for the teeming life which is surrounding Biswas in the overcrowded house. Eventually, Biswas himself, dying slowly from a heart disease, recalls the blighted trees, poisoned from within, for 'his complexion grew dark: not the darkness of a naturally dark skin, not the darkness of sunburn; this was a darkness that seemed to come from within, as though the skin was a murky but transparent film and the flesh below it had been bruised and become diseased and its corruption was rising' (p. 529).

So the final triumph, the acquisition of the house, seems short-lived, as Biswas dies slowly, petulant and querulous, estranged from his son Anand, whose comprehension and love is the thing he needs most in the world. But (p. 530),

> . . . right at the end everything seemed to grow bright. Savi returned and Mr Biswas welcomed her as though she were herself and Anand combined. Savi got a job, at a bigger salary than Mr Biswas could ever have got; and events organised themselves so neatly that Savi began to work as Mr Biswas ceased to be paid. Mr Biswas wrote to Anand: 'How can you not believe in God after this?' It was a letter full of delights. He was enjoying Savi's company; she had learned to drive and they went on little excursions; it was wonderful how intelligent she had grown. He had got a Butterfly orchid. The shade was flowering again; wasn't it strange that a tree which grew so quickly could produce flowers with such a sweet scent?

For the tree which eventually grows true and straight, and produces fragrant flowers, is Savi herself, and it is her unexpected blossoming that crowns Biswas' life with success. Biswas dies, but the house he has provided for his children is like a garden in which they can grow and flourish, and the measure of his triumph is that this bower becomes, for them, ordinary, and all the former halting places recede into the memory, to return only in the future under the passing stimulus of an apparently unrelated incident or impression. 'A fragment of forgotten experience would be dislodged, isolated, puzzling ... When the memories had lost the power to hurt, with pain or joy, they would fall into place and give back the past' (pp. 523-4). So, Mr Biswas transcends the limitations of time and space—his apparently crushing environment—and lives beyond death in the minds of Anand and Savi.

From 'Theme and Image in V. S. Naipaul's *A House for Mr Biswas'*, *Texas Studies in Literature and Language*, VIII (Winter 1967), pp. 589-602 (594-7, 600-2).

NOTE

1 Krikler, B. 'The Novel Today: V. S. Naipaul's *A House for Mr Biswas'*, *The Listener*, 13 February 1964, p. 270.

KENNETH RAMCHAND

The Vision of a 'Sustaining Community' in Claude McKay's *Banana Bottom*

... Bita Plant, the daughter of a Jamaica peasant, is brought up by the Reverend Malcolm Craig and his wife Priscilla. After seven years abroad at an English university and on the Continent, Bita returns to her native land. *Banana Bottom* (New York and London, 1933) tells the story of how Bita gradually strips away what is irrelevant in her English upbringing, and how she marries Jubban, the strong silent drayman in her father's employ.

... The action of the novel alternates between the village of Banana Bottom where Bita spends her early years, and the adjoining town of Jubilee where she is groomed by the Craigs; and McKay makes unobtrusive use of the nominal difference between the two in order to symbolize Bita's final liberation and embrace of the folk. But our first impression is of community:

> That Sunday when Bita Plant played the ɪ old straight piano to the singing of the Coloured Choristers in the beflowered school-room was the most exciting in the history of Jubilee.
>
> Bita's homecoming was an eventful week for the folk of the tiny country town of Jubilee and the mountain village of Banana Bottom. For she was the only native Negro girl they had ever known or heard of who had been brought up abroad. Perhaps the only one in the island. Educated in England—the mother country as it was referred to by the Press and official persons. (p. 1)

The communal memory is of specific times and specific events, '*That* Sunday when Bita played'; it has its landmarks, its familiar items and its own institutions—'*the* ... schoolroom ... *the* ... piano' and '*the* Coloured Choristers'. The private experience, 'Bita's homecoming', is also an event for the folk. In the second paragraph the authorial voice glides mimetically into the communal voice. From these opening moments of the novel McKay steadily builds up a sense of a way of life. Its constitutive elements are tea-meeting, picnic, market, harvest festival, pimento picking, house-parties and ballad-making. Its people range themselves across an ordered spectrum of swiftly and vividly drawn individuals: Squire Gensir, the Englishman in exile; Reverend and Mrs Craig, the missionaries with a civilizing purpose; Belle Black, the village free-living maid and her friend Yoni Legge; Tack Tally and Hopping Dick, the village dandies; Kojo Jeems and Nias Black, drummers; Phibby Patroll, the roving gossip; Herald Newton Day, the pompous theological student, local boy groomed by the Craigs for stardom with Bita; Crazy Bow, the wondering flute boy; the Lambert brood on the weary road to whiteness; the mulatto Glenleys, and Wumba the obeah man.

The main action takes place against a background buzzing with life and implication. But it is more than this. Bita belongs to a sustaining community just as a Naipaul character sticks incongruously out of a crowded depressing canvas. It is because Bita belongs, and because the community is realized as having spontaneous values of its own, that we can credit her fictional process. The incident with Crazy Bow which leads to Bita's adoption by the Craigs illustrates how McKay enriches the background life of the community by drawing out one of the background characters to perform a specific significant function and then letting him slip back into his independent life again.

... Crazy Bow the harmless idiot often frisks with Bita by the riverside. As they do one Saturday:

> As they romped, Bita got upon Crazy Bow's breast and began rubbing her head against his face. Crazy Bow suddenly drew himself up and rather roughly he pushed Bita away and she rolled off a little down the slope.
>
> Crazy Bow took up his fiddle, and sitting under a low and shady guava tree he began to play. He played a sweet tea-meeting love song. And as he played Bita went creeping upon her hands and feet up the slope to him and listened in the attitude of a bewitched being.
>
> And when he had finished she clambered upon him again and began kissing his face. Crazy Bow tried to push her off. But Bita hugged and clung to him passionately. Crazy Bow was blinded by temptation and lost control of himself and the deed was done.
> (p. 10)

The setting is idyllic. Bita is drawn like a natural creature 'creeping upon her hands and feet up the slope to him' and Crazy Bow is involuntarily possessed. The incident does not call for a moralising gloss. The ballad-makers put it into 'a sugary ditty' (p. 14). The stabilising community absorbs and transforms the deed 'and soon the countryside was ringing' with songs:

You may wrap her up in silk,
You may trim her up with gold,
And the prince may come after
To ask for your daughter,
But Crazy Bow was first. (p.15)

This is one of the ways in which McKay suggests the distinctive value of the Banana Bottom society but there is an attempt to use the incident in a more explicit way. We are returning, to the question of how presented life in fiction relates to authorial theory.

Burning to deliver herself of the news, Sister Phibby Patroll travels the fifteen miles from Banana Bottom to Jubilee by foot. Her overnight trek gives her a decisive lead:

> So Sister Phibby told the tale to Priscilla Craig. And although she thought it was a sad thing as a good Christian should, her wide brown face betrayed a kind of primitive satisfaction as in a good thing done early. Not so that of Priscilla Craig's. It was a face full of high-class anxiety, *a face that generations upon generations of Northern training in reserve, restraint, and Christian righteousness have gone to cultivate, a face fascinating in its thin benevolent austerity.* (pp. 15-16; my italics)

For much of *Banana Bottom*, McKay expresses cultural dualism not by setting up explicit contrasts but by celebrating the Banana Bottom community. This is why it is possible to read the work as a serene evocation of the loved place. In this passage, however, McKay does not resist the temptation to make an easy hit. It is plausible enough that Sister Phibby should show the kind of satisfaction McKay describes—and the satisfaction derives from Sister Phibby's understanding of what is likely to be Mrs Craig's view on the subject. But in the section I have italicized McKay seems to be stating his case according to an authorial preconception of prejudice about a type and not in relation to the individual character in the interview. The whole is re-done with much less self-consciousness and with great effect a few lines later:

> 'Poor child!' said Priscilla Craig.
> 'Yes, poor child,' echoed Sister Phibby .... 'But she was oberwormanish ob a ways the folkses them say.'
> 'That's no reason she should have been abused,' said Priscilla Craig.
> 'Temptation, Missis,' sighed Sister Phibby, 'and the poor fool was mad! What kyan a poah body do ag'inst a great big temptation?'
> 'Pray to God, of course, Sister Phibby,' said Mrs Craig. (p. 16)

The conversation comes close to the truth of the presented incident. And the Banana Bottom ethic proves to be a more flexible one than that represented by Mrs Craig. It does so simply by being itself.

The Crazy Bow incident establishes Bita's natural connection with the Banana Bottom world. Her transference to Jubilee and tutelage under the Craigs is an artificial thing. When Bita returns after her seven years abroad she is still herself. The character who is a returned native presents McKay with a plausible medium for the nostalgia expressed in his poems and in the earlier novels. Bita goes to the market. McKay describes the wealth of the land collected in one place and records the sounds and sights of the haggling scene. Then:

> Bita mingled in the crowd, responsive to the feeling, the colour, the smell, the swell and press of it. It gave her the sensation of a reservoir of familiar kindred humanity into which she had descended for baptism. She had never had that big moving feeling as a girl when she visited the native market. And she thought that if she had never gone abroad for a period so long, from which she had become accustomed to viewing her native life in perspective, she might never have had the experience....
> The noises of the market were sweeter in her ears than a symphony. Accents and rhythms, movements and colours, nuances that might have passed unnoticed if she had never gone away, were now revealed to her in all their striking detail. And of the foodstuff on view she felt an impulse to touch and fondle a thousand times more than she wanted to buy. (p. 41)

But this is not simply plausible nostalgia, it is part of a dramatic process that is to end with the marriage of Bita to her father's drayman.

... The clash between Bita and Mrs Craig is successfully dramatized as a particular one between two incompatible people ... [It] develops into a confrontation between two ways of life. Instead of the rhetoric of an authorial voice (as so often in the earlier novels), we move here into the consciousness of a character seeking a *modus vivendi*:

> Bita retired to her room. And the more she thought of the incident the more resentful she became. She wondered now that she had come home to it after all the years of training, if she would be able to adjust herself to the life of the mission. (p. 45)

With matters thus poised, the scene shifts from the town of Jubilee to the lush village of Banana Bottom for the week of festivities beginning with the celebration of Emancipation Day.

It is thirty years before Great Gort and Jack O'Lantern and before the march to Independence Square in George Lamming's *Season of Adventure*, so we have to do with Nias Black and Kojo Jeems:

> ... Kojo Jeems, the drummer, had a fine set of drums and he was loved for his wonderful rattling of the kettle-drum. His son beat the big drum. They went playing down the hill followed by a few ragged kiddies, to the hub of the village. There they were joined by the fiddler and the flute-blower and played and played, with the sun mounting higher and hotter, until there was gathered together a great crowd. And all marched swaying to the music over the hill, and picking up marchers marking time along the wayside, up to the playground. (p. 63)

At the picnic on Table Top Plateau, McKay's feel for the dialect and his vivid sense of people swiftly contribute to our impression of a known and bounded world.

> First among the rum-shop fellows was Tack Tally proudly wearing his decorations from Panama: gold watch and chain of three strands, and a foreign gold coin attached to it as large as a florin, a gold stick-pin with a huge blue stone, and five gold rings flashing from his fingers. He had on a fine bottle-green tweed suit with the well-creased and deep-turned pantaloons called peg-top, the coat of long points and lapels known as American style. And wherever he went he was accompanied by an admiring gang. (p. 66)

Contained in the Banana Bottom world too are the 'Misses Felicia, Elvira and Lucinda Lambers ... cashew-brown daughters of the ebony parson. They were prim of manners, precise and halting of speech as if they were always thinking while talking that they were the minister's daughters' (p. 65). It is a world of gossip and ballad and anecdote. But it is a world whose laws are framed from the outside. Bita explains to the exiled Englishman Squire Gensir that her function at the mission prevents her from dancing and from attending tea-meetings. Gensir nevertheless persuades her to attend Kojo Jeems's tea-meeting. Under this unofficial teacher's tutelage, Bita's rebellion begins. At Kojo's tea-party Bita looks at the dancers and declares, 'I'm going to join them'; about possible disapproval, 'Oh, I don't care anyhow.' Wilfully she begins:

> ... And Bita danced freely released, danced as she had never danced since she was a girl at a picnic at Tabletop, wiggling and swaying and sliding along, the memories of her tomboyish

girlhood rushing sparkling over her like water cascading over
one bathing upon a hot summer's day.

The crowd rejoiced to see her dance and some girls stood
clapping and stamping to her measure and crying: 'Dance, Miss
Bita, dance you' step! Dance, Miss Bita, dance away!' And she
danced forgetting herself, forgetting even Jubilee, dancing down
the barrier between high breeding and common pleasures under
her light stamping feet until she was one with the crowd. (p. 84)

The roving reporter Phibby Patroll takes the news to Jubilee and
Bita's second clash with Mrs Craig occurs. The consequences are
softened by Bita's use of Gensir's chaperoning name but the Craigs
decide to speed up their plans for Bita's marriage with Herald
Newton Day, the local boy being groomed at the Tabernacle
Theological College.

. . . Bita's conflicts with Mrs Craig and her antagonism to Herald
Newton Day are associated with her alienation from the town of
Jubilee, and with her increasing preference for the village of
Banana Bottom where she had spent her early childhood. She
spends more and more time in the village. 'It was so much
pleasanter and freer at Banana Bottom' (p. 161). A number of
images of immersion associated with constitutive elements of
village life or with the landscape impress her belonging to Banana
Bottom. An example of the former is her dance at Kojo Jeems's
tea-meeting. The latter illustrates incidentally the way in which
McKay is able to make maximum dramatic use of the nostalgia
felt by some West Indian writers who are abroad. On a visit to
Banana Bottom, Bita wanders through her childhood haunts:

> All of her body was tingling sweet with affectionate feeling for
> the place. For here she had lived some of the happiest moments
> of her girlhood, with her school-mates and alone. Here she had
> learned to swim, beginning in the shallow water of the lower end
> with a stout length of bamboo. She remembered how she screamed
> with delight with her school-mates cheering and clapping their
> hands that day when she swam from one bank to the other.
> She slipped off her slight clothes and plunged into the water
> and swam round and round the hole. Then she turned on her
> back to enjoy the water cooling on her breasts. Now she could
> bear the sun above burning down. (p. 117)

The unpretentious manner in which this passage suggests Bita's
belonging and her exultation is best brought out by a comparison
with the poverty of declaration in the closing sentences of Neville
Dawes's *The Last Enchantment* (London, 1960): 'I was a god
again, drunk on the mead of the land, and massive with the sun

chanting in my veins. And so, flooded with the bright clarity of my acceptance, I held this lovely wayward island, starkly, in my arms' (p. 288).

Bita's increasing sense of her rootedness in the Banana Bottom community is reflected in her deliberate flouting of Mrs Craig's wishes. A climax of a kind is reached when, with Herald Newton long banished, the two women clash over Hopping Dick's coming to the mission to escort Bita to a dance. Mrs Craig wants to know if Bita loves Dick. Bita says she could love him.

> 'A low peacock,' said Mrs. Craig, 'who murders his h's and altogether speaks in such a vile manner—and you an educated girl—highly educated.'
> 'My parents also speak broken English,' said Bita.
> Anger again swept Mrs Craig and a sharp rebuke came to her lips, but it was checked when her eyes noted Bita toying enigmatically and ostentatiously with Herald Newton's engagement ring on her finger. (p. 210)

Moving from this particular show of antagonism between the two characters, and with the weight of similar demonstrations in earlier episodes behind him, McKay enters the consciousness of Bita:

> Bita was certain now that the time had arrived for her to face the fact of leaving Jubilee. It would be impossible for her to stay when she felt not only resentment, but a natural opposition against Mrs Craig. A latent hostility would make her always want to do anything of which Mrs Craig disapproved. Bita could not quite explain this strong feeling to herself. It was just there, going much deeper than the Hopping Dick affair. Maybe it was an old unconscious thing now manifesting itself, because it was to Mrs Craig, a woman whose attitude of life was alien to hers, and not to her parents, she owed the entire shaping of her career. (p. 211)

The passage is a crucial one in the sense that the doctrine it contains plays a part in the conception of the novel but it is also crucial in terms of Bita's growing self-awareness. The flat declaration of an attitude which we have just seen in action is followed by the tentative 'could not quite explain' and 'maybe', groping for an explanation, and then a resolution repeated, 'Bita knew that she was going to go', which leads into a wave of disgust and an assertive action:

> She became contemptuous of everything—the plan of her education and the way of existence at the mission, and her eye

wandering to the photograph of her English college over her bed,
she suddenly took and ripped it from its frame, tore the thing up
and trampled the pieces under her feet . . . (p. 212)

It is a much more convincing and suggestive process than McKay's
generalisation in *Home to Harlem* that 'civilisation is rotten'. It
is a difference between understanding through art, and becoming
constricted through polemics.

After this comes the routing of Hopping Dick by Aunty Nommy
and the curing of Bita's infatuation: more in antagonism to Mrs
Craig than as a result of her feelings for the dandy, Bita, 'bold as
a lioness', declares she wants to marry Dick; the shifty vagabond
cannot envisage a Mrs Hopping Dick and slinks away from Bita's
life. Bita's final return to Banana Bottom in the third year of the
drought coincides unobtrusively with the Revival headed by Evan
Vaughan. In a manner anticipatory of Andrew Salkey's *A Quality
of Violence* (1959), McKay correlates the parched and barren land
with a dryness and violence in the lives of the people.

Squire Gensir takes Bita to one of the Revivalist meetings. But
just outside the church a more primitive drumming cult draws the
congregation. To frenzied drum and swelling chorus the leader
bounces faster and faster then collapses in ecstatic exhaustion:

A woman of the band stepped forth with her supple-jack and
began whipping the fallen leader while the singing rose upon
jubilant notes and others began rolling and jumping. And when
the woman moaned and murmured under the supple-jacking the
people said that the sounds were the voice of the Spirit . . . .
   In the midst of them Bita seemed to be mesmerised by the
common fetish spirit . . . Magnetized by the spell of it, Bita was
drawn nearer and nearer into the inner circle until with a shriek
she fell down. A mighty shout went up and the leading woman
shot out prancing around Bita with uplifted twirling supple-jack,
but a man rushed in and snatched her away before she could
strike. (pp. 249-50)

It would be foolish to confuse Bita with Fola of George Lamming's
Season of Adventure (1960). Fola's season of adventure begins
with her mesmerization at the ceremony of the souls. Bita's mesmerization occurs at the journey's end to confirm her utter
intimacy with the folk. Bita's rescuer was Jubban. A rapid build-up
of this character whose presence McKay had kept skilfully on the
edge of our consciousness throughout the novel is followed by a
logical marriage between the two. The final chapter takes us three
years into the future where we learn that the marriage has been
blessed, the land has prospered under Jubban's hand and that

Jubban's latent qualities have developed in the new context. Bita herself is fulfilled: 'Her music, her reading, her thinking were the flowers of her intelligence and he the root in the earth upon which she was grafted, both nourished by the same soil' (p. 313). In the final scene Aunty Nommy has just struggled to bring young Jordan away from under the mango tree where since dawn he has been gorging himself on ripe fruit:

> 'What a pickney, though! What a pickney!' Aunty Nommy was saying and playfully slapping little Jordan's bottom. 'Showin' you' strengt a' ready mi li't' man. Soon you'll be l'arnin' for square you' fist them off at me.'

In the world of *Banana Bottom*, life is going on.

I have been trying to describe Bita as a highly credible fictional heroine, and we have been seeing her escape from the world of the Craigs into the world of Banana Bottom as a plausibly organized dramatic process. This argues that *Banana Bottom* is a well-made novel. This is one way in which it is like McKay's sonnet 'The Harlem Dancer'. The inevitability of Bita's movement, however, cannot fail to strike the reader. The heroine has always belonged to Banana Bottom: '. . . whatever I was trained like or to be, I know one thing. And that is that I am myself' (p. 100). It is for this reason that Bita's process has been described as self-assertion rather than self-discovery.

To explain the tension we nevertheless feel in reading *Banana Bottom*, and to pin-point the significance of the novel, it is necessary to return to the acts of revolt: their intensity is out of proportion to the threat represented by the world of the Craigs, and they pass beyond assertion to culminate in protective self-surrender. At Kojo Jeems's tea-party Bita 'danced forgetting herself, forgetting even Jubilee, dancing down the barrier between high breeding and common pleasures under her light stamping feet until she was one with the crowd' (p. 84). But it is the episode at her childhood pool that best illustrates what I mean:

> She slipped off her slight clothes and plunged into the water and swam round and round the hole. Then she turned on her back to enjoy the water cooling on her breasts. Now she could bear the sun above burning down. How delicious was the feeling of floating! To feel that one can suspend oneself upon a yawning depth and drift, drifting in perfect confidence without the slightest intruding thought of danger. (p. 117)

Jubban the drayman is a figure of protectiveness (he fights on Bita's behalf, and he saves her from rape). When 'Bita became conscious of the existence of her father's drayman for the first time, she remarked his frank, broad, blue-black and solid jaws and thought it was all right for her father to have confidence in him' (p. 115). Submission and protection predominate in the coming together of Bita and Jubban in the presence of her father's dead body:

> Jubban slackened the reins, hitching them upon a stanchion, and the mules marched slowly along of their own volition and Bita in Jubban's embrace was overwhelmed with a feeling as if she were upon the threshold of a sacrament and she yielded up herself to him there in the bed of the dray. It was strange and she was aware of the strangeness that in that moment of extreme sorrow she should be seized by the powerful inevitable desire for love which would not be denied. (p. 299)

The recurrent McKay experience of malaise, of being born 'out of time' or of being, like the subdued Harlem dancer, perfect in a strange discordant place is the underlying impulse of *Banana Bottom*. It shows through in image or expressive incident. But the achievement of the artist in this work lies in the dispersal of malaise. In *A House for Mr Biswas*, Mr Biswas' self-assertion takes the form of withdrawal. Bita Plant's self-assertion takes the form of immersion. Art reveals possibilities. Reflecting on Blake's 'The Little Black Boy' (quoted in the novel) Bita revels in the thought 'when he from white and I from black cloud free'. It strikes her as 'cutting its way like lightning across the chaos of the human mind, holding the spirit up, aloft, providing poetry the purest sustenance of life, scaling by magic and all the colours of passion the misted heights where science cannot rise and religion fails and even love is powerless' (p. 268). Mr Naipaul's observed Tulsi world is a copy of a world from which it is necessary to escape. In *Banana Bottom*, Claude McKay imagined a community to which it is possible to belong.

From 'Claude McKay and *Banana Bottom*', *Southern Review*, vol. 4 (1970), pp. 53-66 (54-8, 60-6).

EDWARD BRATHWAITE

Roger Mais's *Brother Man* as Jazz Novel

... Our concern in this study is with the novel as an expression of West Indian 'creole' experience: a structure taking its form from the pressures of West Indian social reality. My thesis is that faithfulness to this concern discovers a form similar to that evolved by the American negro in jazz; and ... I hope to be able to trace a working out of this in ... Roger Mais's *Brother Man*.

Brother Man, significantly, opens with a 'Chorus of People'—musical and social elements:

> The tongues in the lane clack-clack almost continuously, going up and down the full scale of human emotions, human folly, ignorance, suffering, viciousness, magnanimity, weakness, greatness, littleness, insufficiency, frailty, strength. They clack on street corners, where the ice-shop hangs out a triangular red flag, under the shadow of overhanging buildings that lean precariously, teetering across the dingy chasm of the narrow lane ...
>
> They clack where the neighbours meet in the Chinese grocery shop on the corner, leaning elbows against the counter with its saltfish odour and the spilled rice grains and brown sugar grains ...
>
> Behind the pocked visage and the toothless grin, behind the wrinkled skin gathered and seamed around the lips and under the eyes, behind the facade of haltness and haleness and cursing and laughter, slander lurks in ambush to take the weakest and the hindmost, and the tongues clack upon every chance ... (1954 edn, pp. 7-8)

This is the basic rhythm of the book. But playing against it, leaking tension into it (compare the method with, say, Vic Reid's *New Day*), there is a staccato counterpoint:

> —Cordy's man get tek-up fo' ganga ...
> — Bra Man show de gospel way ...
> — Me-gal still wi' hold wid Bra' Ambo ... (p.8)

But after this 'downbeat', this introductory statement of theme, the rhythm changes, as it shifts and changes in jazz, and we hear the entry of the first solo instrument—or rather solo instruments, because two people, a woman and a man (Girlie and Papacita), are involved:

> Girlie was idly turning the pages of a magazine when Papacita came in through the door. She did not look up. He closed the door quietly—too quietly—behind him, without taking his eyes off her, came cat-footing across the room . . . (p. 9)

Gradually, as from within a New Orleans ensemble or a Duke Ellington structure, these two solo instruments begin an interchange: the male voice and action (trumpet) alone first, staccato, challenging the female (clarinet):

> Something tickled him at the back of his throat. He wanted to cough.
> He said: *'Hm!'* trying to clear it.
> She turned the page slowly, put her other hand up to her back-hair.
> He went past her, across to the window overlooking the lane, threw it open with a bang, and said, angrily: 'It's like a furnace in here.'
> She went on turning the pages of the magazine she held across her knee. She put a finger up to her lips, wet the tip of it with her tongue, raised her eyes slowly to look at him, as though aware of his presence for the first time, saw him without recognition, without change of expression, and brought her eyes back slowly to the page.
> He leaned against the window and stood looking at her a moment, shrugged, turned away, went across to the bed, sat down, started pulling off his shoes.
> 'Lousy bum,' she said, casually, as though she was speaking to herself, just turning her thoughts out of air.
> 'What's it?' he said.
> But when he looked up, quickly, challengingly, ready to get on with it, she wasn't looking at him at all. (pp. 9-10)

In the next scene (pp. 12-15) another 'duet' is started, this time between a small boy, Joe, and Jennings, a policeman; both, as Mais reveals later, having significant connections with Papacita and Girlie of the first theme. The third theme, also in duet form, introduces two sisters, Cordy and Jesmina (pp. 15-17). And before the introduction of the main character, Brother Man himself, Mais links Girlie-Papacita and Cordy-Jesmina (p. 16), and brings about the expected resolution of 'conflict' between Girlie and Papacita started in the first theme. This resolution is expressed not only as 'plot', as a literal union of voices; the two individual soloists begin to interchange with each other in a kind of collective improvisation. That is, the solo voices (pronoun notes), instead of being continued to separate prargraphs, now begin to appear together in the same lines:

'What you doing over by the window?' she said. 'You gone to sleep?'

He grunted two syllables that said nothing at all.

She started singing softly to herself.

She stooped down, picked up some crumbs from the floor, straightened, looked down at the boards under her feet, went behind the door for the broom.

He watched her sweeping, tidying, making the room like new, without letting *her* know that *he* was watching *her*; *he* watched *her* every movement, feeling deep down that hunger for *her* that kept *him* coming back after every escapade ... *She* was dusting the further end of the room, working gradually over to where *he* was ... (pp. 21-2, my italics)

The introduction of the 'sexual' here is not gratuitous as it is in so many novels (even though Mais is not without the simplicities that these scenes so often seem to attract: 'He watched her like a cat watching a mouse .... The old passion for her came up inside him, made the inside of his mouth seem dry. He pressed his tongue up against the roof of his mouth, brought down some saliva with it' (p. 22)). First and foremost it represents here a union in the fullest sense of the word. It also underlines the social theme of the novel with its emphasis on collectiveness, cohesion and making: 'He watched her sweeping, tidying, *making the room like new* ....' But perhaps most importantly, this scene serves as an introduction and counterpoint to the other and main theme of the book: Brother Man with his sense of spiritual love; and the conflict, within him, as within all men, of this with the physical.

Brother Man sat at his cobbler's bench before the open window looking out upon the lane ...

He was of medium height, medium build. The hair crisped and curled all about his head, around his mouth, over his chin.

When he looked up from his work his eyes pin-pointed the light, and you could see almost all of his pupils. He had a far-away, searching look, as though the intensity of his being came to focus in his eyes ...

He had now, as he always did, an open Bible on the stool beside him ... (p. 22)

After this short introduction, Brother Man's trumpet is joined
by Minette's clarinet in the usual Mais duet pattern, bringing in
the second set of variations on the theme of love:

> He was putting heels to a pair of slippers, and Minette sat on a
> lower stool, at his feet, blacking a pair of shoes. Every now and
> then she stole a glance at him, and went back to blacking the
> shoes again . . .
>   From the yard next door came the sound of someone singing,
> 'Jesu, lover of my soul . . .'
>   She said suddenly, 'What is love?' (p. 23)

And while Brother Man, rather clumsily, tries to answer this
in his own 'spiritual' terms (p. 23), Girlie and Papacita provide
a different answer:

> And now for the first time since they clinched there was a sound
> between them. She laughed, and their mouths met in a savage
> kiss, and she took his bottom lip between her teeth and bit down
> on it until she tasted blood. And she laughed again when his face
> shuddered away from hers, and she said: 'Hurt me like that—
> hurt me—Love me and hurt me! Hurt me hard!' (p. 29)

Brother Man had ended his first exchange with Minette ('He put
his hand out and touched her arm') with 'Peace and love' (p. 27).
But what we see here is not only a natural resolution of tension
between 'physical' Papacita and Girlie. It is also, in a way, a
representation of the way Minette basically feels for Brother Man.
But Minette's reactions, confronted with Brother Man's kind of
love, are more subtle than this. And to make this point and also to
indicate the delicacy and tenuousness of Brother Man's own
position, Mais now moves from clumsy *word* to dramatic *symbol*.
And herein lies his integrity as a 'folk' artist. He is able, always,
to reinforce what is often quite banal verbalisation with meaningful
image:

> 'Did Jesus talk it that way, that what you mean, Bra' Man?'
>   He nodded his head, gravely. 'He give us that word, sister:
> peace an' love.'
>   A bird flew smack into the window glass with a dull thud. It
> fell to the ground outside with a faint cry, stunned with the
> impact.
>   Brother Man got up, with a murmured exclamation, went out
> through the door, and presently came back with the bird in his
> hand. It fluttered a little, scared, though scarcely conscious,
> almost dead. A single drop of blood congealing at the side of

its beak glowed like a jewel against the dark grey-green of its feathers.

It was going to die, Minette knew it, and she had an instant impatience and vexation with Brother Man for trying to bring it back, to make it live. She didn't know why she felt this, only knew that it came up inside her, until she wanted to cry out to him . . .

She watched him as he stood there, holding the bird in his cupped hand, his head bowed over it.

'Don't trouble you'self over it, Bra' Man,' she said, 'it not goin' to live.' (pp. 25-6)

This trapped fluttered bird is Minette, is Brother Man, is all the people who live within this novel. It is also the life of Brother Man's spirit, it is the life of 'making the room new' and it is also the life and love within Minette: 'But she was young, and things were *stirring* inside her, and she couldn't make him understand, or aware of her in that way at all' (p. 32, my italics). The whole novel, in fact, is structured around this image as a jazz improvisation is based on the few notes of a theme.

In the first place, as a matter of pure fact, Rastafarians believe that certain categories of life are sacred. Samuel Elisha Brown made this point in his 'Treatise on the Rastafarian Movement', which appeared in *Caribbean Studies* (Puerto Rico, 1966), vol. 6, no. 1, pp. 39-40:

We are those who obey strict moral and divine laws, based on the Mosaic tenet:

(1) We strongly object to sharp implements used in the desecration of the figure of Man, e.g. trimming and shaving, tattooing of the skin, cuttings of the flesh.

(2) We are basically vegetarians, making scant use of certain animal flesh yet outlawing the use of swine's flesh in any form, shell fishes, scaleless fishes, snails etc.

In *Brother Man* (Brother Man is a Rasta), this point is made with the bird:

'It's dead,' she said . . .

But he still held the little dead body cupped in his hand, as though he could not bear to part with it.

'What you goin' to do with it, Bra' Man?' . . .

'Why you want to keep it before you? Why you don't throw it outside?'

'It is one of God's creatures, and it was alive a little while back, and now it is dead, an' it didn't do no harm. Let it rest there, eh?' he said. (p. 26)

A little later, the boy, Joe, looks in through Brother Man's window and sees the dead bird. 'You want it?' he asks Brother Man:

'Eh?'

'Say if you want it, sah. If you don't want it fo' you'self, please you could give it to me?'

'What you goin' to do with it, son?'

'Cook it, sah.'

Brother Man looked at him, through the torn shirt at the thin wasted belly, without a word he reached out and put the bird in the boy's hand ...

'It is such a little bird,' said Brother Man.

'Nightingale, sah. Eat sweet.'

'Eh?'

'It eat sweet, sah. Good eatin' bird dem.'

'Ah,' said Brother Man.

He looked at the boy, and their eyes met and held.

Brother Man said, as though he had weighed the matter in his mind and had come to a decision: 'I guess that's all right, son.'
(p. 30)

Sometime later there occurs the first variation on this scene; this time made more explicit, and executed in a story-telling myth-making form. (A post-Mais writer would no doubt attempt this in a more accurate Jamaican dialect; rather too many Americanisms creep into *Brother Man*.):

'Say wha' you do dat fo'? Leggo de crab, Ah mean.'

'Crab feel pain, feel 'fraid, same like you an' me.'

'Den you don' eat crab, sah?'

'Eat dem is one t'ing, han'-cuff dem an' ill-treat dem is anodder, son.' :..

'Dem li' crabs got feelin' same as we, mean to say? Gee, Ah sure never thought of dat 'tall, 'tall.'

'Sure is de trut', son ... every li' beanie-bird, every li' crab ... not a-one but God made dem, same's you an' me.'

'An' crablice too, an' ging-gie flies ...?'

Bra' Man frowned. 'Dat's de devil's work, when he broke loose from hell, an' went ravenin' about de world, befo' dey chain him again and t'row him down in the pit.'

The boy, mouth-breathing, looking earnestly into his face, whispered, 'Gee!'

'Be'lze'bub is de god of flies, son, all dem creatures belong to him; but Michael hog-tie him, t'row him down eena pit widout bottom, long long time 'fo' God mek man in de world.'
(p. 73)

'Papacita *blew in through the door, flung his arms wide*, shouted at Girlie, "Get into you' glad-rags, gal, we steppin' out tonight" '
(p. 76, my italics) is another variation on the bird/life/freedom theme; just as this, with Jesmina, is another:

Brother Man was half-soleing a pair of men's hard boots when Jesmina pushed in through the door.

At first sight of her scared, bedraggled appearance, he let the boot he was holding drop to the floor, got up, and started across to her.

For a moment she couldn't speak; just stood there with her hand to her throat.

'What is it, daughter?'

He was beside her now, his arm about her waist. He thought she was going to faint.

'Sit down an' take it easy now, child.' ...

He went and got a thick tweed jacket and drew it around her shoulders ...

She gathered the thick coat about her, clutched between her fingers. She shivered beneath it as though with an ague. (p. 126)

But if the image of the bird symbolises for Mais the hope of life, it also represents the fact of death; and while the various scenes in *Brother Man* counterpoint with each other to help carry the 'story', they also (as with the scene with the bird) carry within themselves the images of both life and death. Girlie biting her lover in orgasm and drawing blood is only one example of this. To represent this duality, in fact, Roger Mais introduces a second Brother—Bra' Ambo—'a powerful obeahman'.

Bra' Ambo himself had given it out that he was 'a higher scientist than Bra' Man, for'—and he washed his hands before him, and smiled smugly—'Bra' Man study de science of de stars, astrology, an' I study de science of de stars too, but I study higher than dat, for I study de science of de Dead.' (p. 84)

From this there follows the most moving scene in the book, the death of Cordy's baby under Brother Ambo's influence. What is artistically interesting about this moment, however, is that it is the icon of the trapped, fluttered bird again, reappearing as an entirely new variation on the original theme. Where we had life, we now find death:

She reached out and pulled the sheet from off the sleeping child.

She shut her eyes, and lifted him up in her arms, pressed his face against her breast. She rocked gently back and forth,

crooning softly above his head, as though hushing him to sleep.
All the time the tiny face was pressed firmly against her breast.
Once the child struggled weakly in her arms, but she held him
still, holding his face close against her bosom. Her own face wore
a blank, shut, almost peaceful expression. She kept her eyes
closed all the time, rocking gently backward and forward,
crooning above his head.
The boy's wasted legs moved, stiffened against her leg. She
didn't heed it, kept rocking him back and forth, crooning,
crooning above his head.
His little hands reached up, clutched weakly at her wrist,
stopped clutching, seemed to falter in their intention, the fingers
folded like the petals of a sensitive flower that had gone to sleep.
His hands lapsed to his sides, his legs ceased their urgent
twitching against her thigh. He lay in her arms perfectly still,
as though he had fallen asleep. (pp. 164-5)

Brother Man, then, reveals certain rhythmic, thematic and structural features which justify, I think, my comparing it to music. Its
specific relationship to New Orleans Jazz comes with its peculiar
sense of union and unity, its contrasting 'duets', its 'improvisation'
and correspondences and above all, its pervading *sense of community* (its *collective* improvisation). The 'Chorus of People' who
introduce each section of the book is only the most obvious
instance of this sense of community—and a rather external instance
at that. Mais's sense of community goes deeper than a mere device.
It informs the very structure of the book.

Brother Man sat at his cobbler's bench before the *open window
looking out upon the lane* ... [p. 22, my italics]
From the yard next door they could hear voices of people,
talking, laughing, quarrelling. Beyond they could hear the yam-
vendor hawking down the lane ... (p. 22)

Everything that happens in this novel has its bearing on these
people, on the community. They know what goes on, they talk about
it, they react to what they know. We get to know them, through their
various representatives, better and better as the novel progresses,
until in the end, through Brother Man, at a moment of grave social
misunderstanding, we come face to face with them ourselves:

Few people were abroad tonight as he took his walk down the
lane. Some youngsters, gathered in a close knot on the sidewalk
just at the street intersection, shouted obscenely after him as he
passed: 'Yah! Why you don' shave you' beard!' 'Gwan! you ole
Ras Tafari, you!' ...

People came out, leaned against their gates. They laughed and jeered, and shouted at him going down the street. Some came out from their yards into the lane itself, followed him from a distance, hurling at his back obscenities, insults. 'See one of de Ras Tafari dem!'

'Gwine mek him shave, wait an' see!'

Someone started singing a song that had lately come into vogue:
> Run man wi'dout beard,
> Beard-man after you . . .

Others joined in, they screamed and shouted it after him, tunelessly, down the lane. (p. 183)

With this 'tunelessness', this social ensemble which still retains its sense of unity though at the brink of collapse, we reach that dark and chaos which lies at the heart of jazz:

A great blood-thirsty cry went up from the crowd. Like a pack of wolves they surged in upon him . . .

A woman on the outskirts screamed, rushed forward, threw herself on her knees beside him, tried to shield him with her body. They tore her clothes and roughly threw her aside . . .

The reeking wave of humanity surged over and over him, like a jackal-pack, when one of them is down. (pp. 185-6)

Compare this—solo instrument against the roaring jazz ensemble —'like a jackal-pack, when one of them is down'—making its own greater unity—with a similar scene from, say, John Hearne's *Voices Under the Window*, which I would analyse as a 'non-jazz' novel. Whereas in *Brother Man* the crowd, who have always inhabited the book, finally blare out with a sound of violent self-assertion against a person who is essentially one of themselves, in Hearne's book the crowd is an alien force; and violence comes to the protagonist not from the ensemble, but from a *clearly defined individual*, bringing not creative chaos, but destructive clarity:

. . . a man came out of the crowd suddenly, a thin, good-looking, broad-cheeked mulatto, with his eyeballs as red as coals; he was carrying a heavy, soft-iron machete, the blade dark and smooth except for the edge which was bright silver, with the file scratches plain across it. He came up behind Mark and said, in a low, cold voice of remote madness, 'Put him down, you white bitch.' Then he chopped Mark with the expert, all wrist and forearm driving motion of a man who has cut bananas on a plantation or has killed the beef cattle as they come plunging and terrified out of the slip-gate on the cattle-pens. (p. 18)

The difference between the violence in *Voices Under the Window* and in *Brother Man* is that in the former, the consequent suffering involves and illuminates an individual. In *Brother Man* the violence is a kind of communal purgation. It involves the entire community of the novel, finally moving beyond the apparent chaos it brings, to that revelation of wholeness that one is aware of at the end of a successful jazz improvisation:

> He saw all things that lay before him in a vision of certitude, and he was alone no longer.
> 'Look at me,' he said.
> Her gaze met his, unfaltering.
> 'You see it out there, too?'
> She [Minette] looked up above the rooftops where the great light glowed across the sky.
> She said: 'Yes, John [Brother Man], I have seen it.'
> 'Good,' he said, and again, 'Good.'
> He moved away from the window, back into the cool dimness of the room beyond.
> And she went before him, carrying herself proudly, shielding the little flame of the candle with her hand. (p. 191)

Here, despite the 'exaltation' (Mais's great weakness is naïvety and sentimentality), are resolved the basic conflicting elements of love of the spirit and of the flesh, which are the burden of this book . . . .

From 'Jazz and the West Indian Novel', parts 2 and 3, *Bim*, no. 45 (July-December 1967), pp. 39-51 (51), and no. 46 (January-June 1968), pp. 115-26 (115-24).

JOYCE ADLER

Wilson Harris's *Tumatumari* and the Family of Man

Anyone interested in gaining insight into the nature and potential-
ities of imagination should look deeply into Wilson Harris's
Tumatumari (Faber, 1968). This eighth of Harris's extraordinary
novels reveals his unusually original imagination at its present high
state of development—a height to which it has evolved in the
practice of the creative process he described theoretically in his
lectures and essays.

... Imagination is embodied in *Tumatumari* in the 'heroine'
Prudence, this novel's representative of Man. She is the 'soul of
man' awakening in a transitional age that may have already begun,
feeling at last the need to develop and transform itself if the family
of Man is to continue. To understand herself and her needs and
desires, she reaches into memory, the well of the past. The search
for the significance of the history of her own family, a middle-class
'mixed' family in Guyana, leads to an exploration of twentieth-
century civilisation generally, as symbolised by the life of this single
'civilised' family, and expands further into an exploration of the
relationship between the twentieth century in Guyana (the land of
Harris's birth and development) and other times and other places.
Only in this broader search can Prudence find her own real
identity, her identity with the whole human family, its evolutionary
past, its complex present, and its two possible futures, not yet
determined in this 'moment' of history. The implications of
Prudence's search reach out without limit backward in time,
outward without limit into space, and inward from one horizon
of imagination to the next.

The implication is that in *Tumatumari* Harris, too, set out to
put the history of his own family and country together, and that
out of the immersion of his imagination in this material, *Tumatumari*, with its constantly widening implications, developed. For
to Harris, the story of Guyana and its different peoples is charged
with the deepest meanings and the largest questions. Out of his
continuously widening exploration as he created *Tumatumari* came
the questions: Of what contradictory elements is the civilisation of
our age composed? Out of what womb did it come? Is it capable

or incapable of giving birth in its turn? Is civilisation now a totally barren thing truly lusting for self-destruction? If not, is it capable of a new kind of conception, a conception of something new, capable of surviving after its birth, not something born to die like Prudence's child, something that cannot live since it is no more than an extension of the primitive past and the still-primitive present? Will the breakdown of life in this century and the consequent sense of the imminence of danger give mankind the necessary humility to surrender long-cherished but long-outworn and now barren concepts and idolatries? Can so-called 'modern Man' bear to face himself as still no more than primitive, living by primitive concepts, still offering living sacrifices to his gods, still sacrificing himself and others in the name of separate 'incestuous' family or nation, tribe or race? Will it be possible, in the terms of the novel, for the early, still-primitive Prudence (caring only about her own family and its story) to be transformed into a new Prudence with a wider meaning to her name? Can the real welfare of 'one's own' and that of others be seen convincingly as indivisible? Can concern for the individual family and concern for the whole human family be fused by imagination, giving birth to an entirely new conception—that of an integrated, unalienated, creative and truly human Man? And, to return to Guyana in a broader, non-national sense, does the Central and South American 'new world', the melting pot of ancient and new, and of many races and cultures, have, perhaps, the best potential for being the crucible of change in the world today?

The interaction of this rich mass of questions and material with Harris's highly-cultivated and informed twentieth-century mind and fluid imagination results in what is undoubtedly one of the most complex novels ever written. Reading and re-reading *Tumatumari* is a gruelling as well as a rewarding experience; it is a rigorous challenge to the reading ability and imagination of the reader.

... The story itself is so many-faceted that it is possible to suggest it only in rough outline. In what can be called the prelude, or overture, Prudence comes down to the river from her house on the hill at Tumatumari, which is deep in the interior of Guyana. The time is just before sunrise, in the moment of suspension between darkness and light. The forest and river are shrouded in mist and the sound of the waterfall is muffled. In the half-light Prudence sees many paths leading to her. She is suffering, empty, groping. Is it lust for self-destruction that she feels or desire for re-creation? She lifts a mat of vegetation from the river's edge and her flesh begins to come to life, 'pregnant with possibilities'.

Suddenly she is back in her room in the house on the hill being cared for by Rakka, her husband's Amerindian servant and mistress, of whom she is of course jealous, although Roi Solman, the husband, is now dead, killed a year after their marriage in a 'collision' at the falls. Their baby too has died. Prudence knows that she has suffered a nervous breakdown, but she feels sure that what she has lifted from the river, the 'One' in her arms, is not a hallucination. (Neither she nor the reader understands what the 'One' is at the time.) Prudence feels there is the possibility of re-creation of herself through a confession of weakness, through humility; what makes it possible for her attitude of self-righteous privilege to give way is that one blow on top of the other has broken her rigidity. She opens her eyes, looks at Rakka, and smiles. Only when the novel is read and re-read does the reader see that Prudence in the prelude is the picture of humanity at this moment of civilisation's crisis, when it must decide whether it has the will to change its conceptions of life in order to survive.

In the main body of the work, in the search for her own significance and real desires, Prudence searches the paths which have led to her. The principal figure in her past is her father, Henry Tenby, head of a Guyanese middle-class family until his death in 1957. He is the novel's symbol of the dominant outlook and way of life of the first half of the twentieth century.

As a young man travelling in Europe shortly after World War I, Tenby has fallen in love with Isabella, the golden 'muse of the century' who attracts him with her 'scent of the chase'. She gives an illusion of beauty and of wealth but in truth she is hungry inside, and without any real substance. Like the seemingly rich century, she is covered in glamorous drapery which hides a body of poverty. In England she vanishes, leaving Tenby with ambivalent feelings of love and hate.

He returns to Guyana in the 1920s, the post-war depression years. There upon an earlier 'Rakka' he conceives three children, years before their actual birth. They are the mental conceptions of Tenby's life, the principles (or lack of them) by which he lives until the moment of his death.

The first to be thus conceived is Prudence (although she is the last actual child, born in 1940). She is conceived mentally while Tenby is shopping for his 'mask of a lifetime' in the 'Brothel of Masks', the place where flesh and blood are devalued and imagination is traded for gold. Tenby's conception is of a narrow prudence. He determines that he will, when he marries, live only for his family. Therefore, he, a historian, vows silence, to protect, as he believes, the welfare of his future family. He will avoid, in his historical accounts, explaining the stranglehold he sees that history has had on Rakka. (The name Rakka is used for a woman in each generation, of one race or another, who is used but neglected, and held in the lowest esteem.)

One with whom the Rakkas are equated is Tenby's son Hugh Skelton (skeleton in the closet) who is the dark-skinned member of this 'civilised' family in Guyana. Hugh is conceived in Tenby's mind in 1924, year of depression and malaria, of strikes, lockouts, riots, the killing of thirteen strikers by the police, and of concern by the taxpayers about the budget! Hugh is 'conceived' in fear, for Tenby is fearful of confrontation with the stark realities of humanity shackled. So out of fear he conceives the ideal of 'refinement' and determines that in his account of the times he will hide all things that are socially unacceptable. Out of the coward's attitude that Tenby adopts comes, as a natural result, the hard life of the actual Hugh Skelton; he is always hidden when company comes because his skin is dark; he has the hardest chores in the family; and he is eventually killed in the riots against the budget in 1962; by a bullet inscribed, 'This bullet fired by your father's rich kith and kin—all races of endeavour—white + brown + black' (p. 120).

Tenby's third 'pre-conception' is his daughter Pamela, the first of these three to be actually born to Tenby and his European-Creole wife Diane, a woman who seems poised and knowledgeable but who is really filled with anxieties and knows nothing. Pamela is conceived—not physically but in abstraction—in 1926, a year of drought, when difficulty and squalor are too much for Tenby to bear. He does not resist measures by the Crown to muffle and disqualify a Popular Party, as later in 1953 he will be apathetic to the suspension by the British of the constitution. His abstraction from the struggles of the day leads to his purely abstract conception of a 'model' of purity and innocence, of perfection supposedly. His daughter Pamela later plays her 'model' role so well that she marries into the affluent society of the United States. (Richardson's novel, *Pamela or Virtue Rewarded*, probably contributed her name.) But in the USA, in order to remain accepted by this 'model' society, Pamela must sacrifice the dark child to whom she too gives birth. Only in this way is she able to escape the US ghetto and live her 'model' life. The sacrifice of the grandchild is the result of Tenby's acceptance of the imposed values of his society.

Of Tenby's three children only Prudence is 'reconceived'—long after her father's death. The seeds of her rebirth are planted at the moment of his death which results from a heart attack following a collision on the road (between head and heart? reality and appearance?) His imagination, on which he has kept reins all his life, now takes over and he becomes at death a 'creature cloven in two, one face on top mask-like as before, the other face beneath emerging from the old' (p. 45). Prudence is alone with him when he staggers into the house. His mask falls—the mask of his age— and she sees the agonised face beneath. It is a traumatic experience for her, but it has beneficial effects years later when she looks back into her past and is able to reconstruct the real meaning of her father's life and time. She is assisted by Tenby's hidden manuscripts he does not have time to destroy.

Prudence comes to understand him as representative of Man in the age of individualism and free enterprise, who is in truth as unfree as possible. Placarded by history as being the soul of freedom, he wears chains of gold upon his heart and wrist. Prudence's feeling for him years later is a feeling of compassion. She sees him as unable to advance far beyond the limits of the past out of which he came. She sees both him and her husband Roi as manifestations of Man in the two major periods of this century, the periods following each of the world wars:

> Each age his expression altered within everything, family as well as nation—cradle as well as grave—crumpled into dust and yet was miraculously restored, rehabilitated by generations of folly, hope. Strange legendary dead and yet unborn spirit he was for each changing day...Never the same. Always the same. (pp. 99-100)

History seems a hopeless business if generation after generation is still chained to the primitive past, but it is not entirely hopeless since the evolutionary process which Harris sees at work in history is one in which sudden leaps occur; and who can tell when there will emerge, 'out of a spring that was poisoned—ONE who had spent but a night beneath the unequal burden of time' (p. 100), and who will be Man reborn, transformed and united.

At the other extreme of the earlier generation (the underprivileged extreme) is the mother of the Amerindian Rakka. She has refused to join her daughter in the house of Roi Solman, the engineer-technologist. She keeps to the old nomadic way. Her life is a life of squalor and her line also seems without a future, since Rakka is thought to be barren. What Rakka's mother has done, however, is 'endure' in both senses of the word: she has endured (suffered) and she has endured (survived). She therefore has something to contribute to the 'One' of the future—a core of strength.

Roi Solman (King Sun-man?), the engineer husband of Prudence, seems to represent the post-World War II period, to 1967. His is the objective, realistic mind. He is intelligent, and learns from experience. In fact, a shock in 1962 (year of the first race conflicts in Guyana) has given him a new insight into the problems of his time. He is capable of recognising the truth about the poor whom he uses in his work, that they have been made use of 'in the name of emancipation, science, industry, all rolled into one—self-interest'

(p. 34). But he tells Prudence not to worry: 'It's too late to change course now. Poverty is our wealth' (p. 34). It is a collision course that he, like our age, is following, but since he does not know how to avoid it, he has developed a sardonic sense of humour to protect himself. His laughter is his attempt to gain immunity from suffering. His clowning absurdity is his fetish against evil. Partly Amerindian, he feels that the Amerindians represent 'the conscience of our age. In this part of the world anyhow'. He admits that he is tormented at the thought of their plight. 'Yet they yield a profit.' He tries to maintain a delicate balance, tries to maintain his supremacy. 'One cannot tolerate breakdown in day to day rule' (p. 36). So, in the name of self-preservation he rubs his nose on the rock, symbol of the 'petrified' (in two senses) establishment.

Roi resembles Tenby in many ways. He too keeps a tight rein on his compassion and imagination. He too acts for Prudence, sacrificing others and himself in her name. He is shown to be like the ancient 'divine king' whose life, it was believed, had to be sacrificed when there came a breakdown in the life of the people. But Harris implies that no such outworn primitive rituals and idolatries can save twentieth-century Man, who must himself accept the responsibility for his fate, not shift it to any god or gods. No sacrifices will help except the sacrifice of outworn conceptions, such as the idea that the world is inevitably made up of hunter and hunted. The only hope of survival lies in more deeply scientific knowledge of nature and its processes and in the renewal of man's own creative power. Man himself must be the creator of the new Man. His future depends on himself.

In her recollections of her husband Prudence sees his role in history as that of both hunter and hunted. He is in pursuit of and pursued by contradictions. She sees him doomed in one sense: 'Doomed to fall she felt: to collide—to be decapitated like an outworn model. To be sublime, however—a forerunner—an outrider of storm ... For the pith and core of his sun lay in illumining a structure of relationships' (p. 81). If Mankind is to be reborn, it will be because he could learn so much from this age.

Last in the cast of this Harris 'drama of consciousness' is the band of Indians Prudence sees early in the novel. They are a primitive South American tribe whom Prudence has hardly known existed, but with whom she senses identity, as gradually she does with all the characters. The Indians' corial on the river (of time) and her house on the hill are 'loci of community ... two points high and low—and yet ... inseparable'. The tribe have lost their original vision; she feels that she has too. When she sees them the second time, they cry to her to be born again through her, 'expelled from the bandage of history'. She—her age—is their last hope. They stop, then plunge to read the summons of life or death. Suddenly, in their life or death is implied the life or death of all, for they too represent not only their own age but mankind and his original sleeping genius, still surviving but in danger of disappearing. The survival of the band of Indians depends on whether she will find and assimilate them and what they mean. They are all that is most alien to this century it would seem, yet something of the spirit they have lost is what she must find or re-discover beneath the blanket of history. Their original fresh vision must be incorporated into her new vision.

In *Tumatumari*, then, the central figure or symbol is Man himself, in his manifestations in various periods in his whole history, during which he has lived in many different societies and within the wider environment of nature—within the womb of space and time. The title of *Tumatumari* derives from the idea of nature and its processes in time ('Tumatumari' is said to mean 'sleeping rocks'). The scene of Tumatumari suggests that in time even rocks crack, and imaginations awaken, and sudden leaps in development take place.

In contrast, the titles of the five sub-divisions of the book derive from social forms and concepts, those that have lasted beyond their time, that once were meaningful, perhaps, but which now are death-dealing. They represent old ideas that can have meaning now not as binding, rock-like traditions and idolatries, but only as 'transformed and transforming' tradition, meaningful for this age. For example, Man's major social preconception of life as the game or the hunt needs to be reconceived. The old concepts may once have had the validity of growing out of their appropriate levels of historical development; they were once not ideas imposed by a dead past on early man but concepts original with him (even if mistaken) and growing out of his own experience. It is the originality and independence of spirit that is still valid and not the long outworn interpretations of life and nature. Today Man needs to evaluate, test, and change 'each given situation' to keep pace, if possible, with life as it changes; he needs to look to the farthest horizon he can perceive from the vantage point of our age. Only such an outlook holds any promise of a future for Man. Rigid adherence to old rock-bound tradition will doom him.

. . . Some of the philosophical implications of the novel raise certain questions in the mind of this reader: Is it possible to see the present crisis of mankind rightly, if we view him as one solid mankind only? Doesn't the use of a single figure like Tenby or Roi to represent mankind in successive ages imply that there is but a single human consciousness and experience in each age? Who, in the recent period, would represent mankind in the age of colonialism—the man of the British middle class, for example, or the man of African origin struggling for freedom in Kenya? Is there not a necessary complementary approach to Harris's anthropological one if we are to see the fullest realities of an age, an approach that shows the movement of history in that age as not only part of the overall rhythm of history, but as the result also of the internal dynamic encounters and interactions of *separate* people or groups of people with often conflicting experiences, consciousnesses and feelings? (This is the reality that *The Waiting Room* illustrated.) And do changes of attitude grow within consciousness or memory without constant interaction between it and the world and events outside it? Tenby and Roi are seen in relationship with the events of their age; why is Prudence portrayed as changing in interaction with memory alone?

But even if this point is valid, that an additional view of history is needed to supplement Harris's view in which mankind is assumed to have a representative consciousness and experience before the unity of man, in this sense, is achieved, yet the question is of minor importance in relation to *Tumatumari* with its stimulating wealth of ideas and the contact it makes possible with Harris's rare mind and imagination and his commitment to Man.

There is a statement by the physicist de Broglie that seems almost meant to apply to this work:

> Often the feeling of the imminence of a danger gives birth in the heart of men to sentiments ... which can serve to avoid it ... Confronted by the dangers ... man has need of a 'supplement of soul' and he must force himself to acquire it promptly before it is too late. It is the duty of those who have the mission of being the spiritual or intellectual guides of humanity to labour to awaken in it this supplement of soul. (*Physics and Metaphysics*, Harper, New York, 1960, p. 264)

It is as if, in *Tumatumari*, the imagination of Wilson Harris is responding to this call.

From '*Tumatumari* and the Imagination of Wilson Harris', *Journal of Commonwealth Literature*, no. 7 (July 1969), pp. 20-31 (20-2, 24-31).

PART IV

A Language of One's Own

R. B. LE PAGE

Dialect in West Indian Literature

It would be possible to discuss this topic from one of three points of view: that of the reader of West Indian literature, that of the writer, and that of the West Indies. I shall consider the question of the writer's use of dialect as a functional tool in West Indian writing. It is not possible wholly to isolate this aspect of the problem from others more intimately associated with the growth of national culture on the one hand, and on the other with the development of receptivity and consciousness towards that culture on the part of the reader. Moreover, I think it necessary and desirable to relate the dilemma of the West Indian writer to the general problem of writers, and indeed of creative artists in any generation and in any country, struggling to find a bridge between the personal language in which they most happily express themselves and the common language of their audience.

An African novelist writing in one of the English papers said that she used more or less standard English for her novels but felt a traitor as she did so. The use of this medium enabled her to reach a very much wider audience, and she felt that perhaps she was contributing to the cultural unity of Africa by writing about her part of Africa in a language which was spoken in many different parts of the continent. But, she said, she drew her inspiration from her native community and felt that she was sucking that community dry and giving nothing back to it in its own vernacular.

Many West Indians bristle slightly (sometimes more than slightly) when I draw an analogy between the situation in the West Indies and that in places where there are vernacular languages quite different from English. However, I think we have now passed the phase which West Indian writers were going through when I first arrived in Jamaica in 1950. Then there was still writing a school of authors who drew their inspiration and their language from the literature of England rather than from life. One cannot deny that this is a perfectly legitimate thing to do and that many in other countries who study English and English literature from a great distance of thousands of miles manage to create for themselves an extraordinarily fertile world of the imagination peopled from that literature, and manage also to write in the language of that literature. Even at its best, however, such writing tends to produce a sense of strain, as it does in Joseph Conrad, because one cannot really write like an Englishman without in some sense becoming an Englishman. The problem is not simply one of geography; it affects also one generation trying to write in the idiom of a former generation. Many people find historical novels unreadable; I do myself as a rule. And the geography need not be a matter of separation by thousands of miles; Robert Burns wrote to a friend in 1794:

> These English songs gravel me to death, I have not that command of the language that I have of my native tongue. In fact, I think my ideas are more barren in English than in Scottish.

It might be helpful if I started by sketching briefly how it is that dialects vary and creole or creolized vernaculars come to be spoken in the West Indies. First, it is important to remember that there is no such thing as a language except in so far as the verbal habits of two or more people overlap. One's verbal behaviour is part of one's total behaviour, but it is a part which is subject to constant social pressures and it is constantly being subjected to modification in order to improve its adequacy as a tool. It is primarily, I think, a means of expression rather than a means of communication; its efficacy as a means of expression depends upon its retaining the imprint of all the formative conditioning which has gone to make one the person one is. Each individual is unique, however, and therefore no two people can be wholly satisfied in their expressive needs by the same set of verbal habits. I have recently been in correspondence with a distinguished French psychologist and linguist, who in her last letter wrote as follows:

> You keep insisting in your notes that each person has his individual language. I feel this is a most important point—and for reasons which are additional to and perhaps more important than those which you have mentioned: we seem to need other people as stimuli to trigger our expression of our own concerns.

In other words, if there is nobody else around, one does not do as much talking as usual not because there is no need to make communication but because there is no triggering mechanism for self-expression. If you feel that language is primarily for communication, make a note next time you are sitting in conversation with your friends of the number of times on which something is said by one and then genuinely taken up and examined and responded to rationally and critically by another. It may seem that I am getting rather away from the topic of dialect as a functional tool in West Indian writing, but I am not. The point is that communication requires the use of *language* (that is, of the area of overlap between two or more people's usage) rather than the use of personal language. Now in order to have an area of overlap you have to decide whom you are going to overlap with. It may be the man next door whose verbal habits are quite similar to yours or it may be a group of people on the other side of the world with whom you have only certain skeletal structures in common. There is a whole range of possibilities in between, but some kind of compromise is necessary. The road along which James Joyce was driving so relentlessly when he wrote *Finnegan's Wake* is a dead end, however brilliantly he explored it and however hopeful that exploration has been.

One's own language is one's response to one's environment; language is a response to environment; language that is transplanted has to respond to the new environment. The group that is transplanted is never exactly the same in composition as any one group in the colonizing country. It is rare for a complete village to be picked up and transported half-way across the world. Even if this happened, contacts in the new situation with speakers of other languages would be different from what contacts would have been if the village had stayed at home. Linguistic change is due mainly to contact; what is not due to contact is due to changes of environment.

In the West Indies we start from the fact that each island was colonized at a different period. The British colonists came from different parts of Britain; at the period when Barbados was settled there was a very high proportion of Irish among them, and in the British end of Montserrat the population was almost entirely Irish to begin with. During the latter part of the eighteenth century in Jamaica, however, the Scots seem to have been numerically the most important British colonists. The African origin of the slaves changed as the patterns of the slave trade changed. To begin with, the Ashanti slaves were the largest single group; then at a slightly later period those from Dahomey; and then the main sources of the trade moved further eastwards along the African coasts so that the Nigerian and Congolese and Angolan slaves came to outnumber very greatly those from the more westerly coasts. In the French West Indian islands, however, the slaves from Dahomey continued to predominate for quite a long period. Then again, the subsequent contacts of the Eastern Caribbean communities have been quite different from those of Jamaica and the Leeward Islands, and those of British Honduras and Guyana have been different again. French has been an important contact in one area, Spanish in another; East Indian languages and American Indian languages have made their influence felt to varying degrees in different places.

The vernaculars spoken in different parts of the West Indies all have in common features which result from interference between West African linguistic habits and English. This interference has taken place at all linguistic levels: phonological, grammatical, lexical and semantic. At the phonological level it has resulted in the pronunciation of vowels and consonants varying and being different from those used in England; it has also resulted in different intonation and stress patterns. Phonology and its relationship to the conventions of the written code are important to the writer since his readers will re-create for themselves (from the signs on the printed page) his voice, or some other voice, silently in their mental ear. We judge people very much by their voices and we judge writers very much from their tone of voice. A great deal of literary criticism nowadays is concerned with interpreting the tone of voice. At the upper levels of scholarship, in mathematics and science, people cultivate a neutral tone of voice or one which simply reveals one as belonging to the university world. Neutrality is no good for the novelist. But if he accurately catches on the printed page the West Indian tone of voice, he has to reckon with the fact that what may sound insulting or ingratiating in one dialect may signal something quite different to speakers of another dialect. At the grammatical level he has to remember that the differences in morphology (for example, the lack of plural endings and past tense endings) are all pretty obvious to people from other parts of the world and to the writer himself, whereas subtle differences of syntax are far less obvious. Syntactic patterns (various word orders, for example) have meanings rather similar to the meaning of words; but may signal different things to different communities.

At the lexical level the writer must realize that he may have quite a different vocabulary in the vernacular he wishes to use from that of other islands, or even where the words are the same and mean the same they may carry quite a different functional load; in other words, people in one region or of one age group may make a great deal of use of a particular part of the vocabulary which is very little used by people of another region and another age group, even though they may be reasonably familiar with that part of the lexicon. And finally, of course, the words may have different meanings from one island to another—the Eastern Caribbean *Akee* is the Jamaican *Guinep*; this is a well known example, but there are hundreds less well known.

The first technical problem, therefore, which the writer has to face is, what variety of West African speech he is going to try to use in his writing. If he uses the parochial dialect with which he is most familiar and perhaps most easily at home in a relaxed manner for telling stories or other intimate purposes he may find that he has only a parochial audience. Once he tries to aim at a slightly larger audience (that, say, of his part of the island, or of his island, or of the Eastern Caribbean, or of the Caribbean as a whole) he enters upon a process of normalization, of finding the ingredients which are common to two or more parochial dialects of West Indian English. Very few of the dialects are bolstered and reinforced by any considerable literature or reference books, although the Jamaican writer now has at his disposal a number of works such as Beryl Loftman Bailey's *Jamaican Creole Syntax* (Cambridge University Press, 1966) and Cassidy and Le Page's *Dictionary of Jamaican English* (Cambridge University Press, 1967). If the writer has travelled widely around the Caribbean he may be sufficiently familiar with all dialects to play it by ear and not need to look anything up; he may be able to find a happy compromise between that parochial dialect in which he is most at home and a variety of West Indian speech so deregionalized as to have lost its characteristic flavour.

I myself believe that there *is* sufficient in common between the creolized English of one part of the Caribbean and another for there to be a potential 'Caribbean English' for writers to use with effect, whatever audience they are aiming at. My feeling about this is based on a number of years of field work with a tape-recorder and subsequently listening to my tapes, made in every part of the Caribbean. I have just completed a book called *English in the Caribbean*, and it contains texts which I have transcribed from these tapes. I have experimented with different spelling systems in an effort to find one which would serve for all territories and help in the production of elementary readers for children which could be used in each territory without losing the characteristic pronunciation of each dialect. This brings me to the next technical difficulty which the writer must face; that is, how is he going to spell the dialect?

A written language is a code which has had a development and has an existence to a certain extent independent of the spoken code to which it is related. We do not just write down what we say; we have to choose a set of conventions for representing speech on paper, we normalize, we restore the abbreviations of speech, we leave much of the intonation and stress to be deduced from the context, while in other ways we are more explicit on paper than in speech because we lack the gestures and the facial expressions which accompany speech. Each convention developed for the eye has its own associations, just as the tone of voice I mentioned earlier has its own associations, and the eye conventions influence the reader in a way rather similar to that in which the ear conventions influence the hearing. If a certain system of spelling has been used in the past for writing down the dialect (and a number of *ad hoc* systems have been used over the past two centuries for this purpose) and if the dialect in the past has been used primarily for humorous recitations and so on, and not for serious literary purposes, then the sight of that spelling system on the printed page is going to mean 'humorous' to the West Indian reader and may well destroy something of the effect at which the writer is aiming. To give an example from England, the spelling 'wot' is commonly used for the word *what* in Cockney dialect, and so means 'Cockney' when it appears on the printed page, even though the pronunciation it represents is no different at all from the pronunciation represented by *what* in educated southern English dialects. Most linguists who have worked on Creole languages have used some kind of phonemic transcription to represent them, and such spelling systems are based on a principle which is very sound from the linguistic point of view: that each significant sound contrast in the language is represented by a contrast between two letters on the printed page and that no letter stands for more than one significant sound. But such transcriptions are often very strange to the lay reader and would alienate him from the writer if they were used in novels. Moreover, in order to use a strictly phonemic writing system it must be based on one particular idiolect; so that the writer who moves linguistically out of his own parish, if he sought to use a phonemic transcription, would be faced with precisely the problem which I have been faced with in trying to find a common writing system for my texts from British Honduras, Nevis, Jamaica, St Vincent and Trinidad.

Once again, therefore, one has to compromise between an accurate representation of one particular dialect and a widely recognizable representation of something general in the West Indies, in a spelling system which does not signal 'comic' but does not on the other hand smack so much of linguistics as to be off-putting to non-linguists. Part of the solution to this problem lies in creating a set of associations for whatever spelling system can be decided upon: once this spelling system has been used several times, the associations which go with it will be those of the writers who have used it, and if they are serious and creative writers the spelling system will no longer be a barrier between them and their audience.

I have mentioned Robert Burns. He did not of course always write in Scots dialect, nor was his representation in a dialect poem consistently of dialect; *The Cotter's Saturday Night* is a curious amalgam of Spenserian stanzas and many conventional eighteenth-century poeticisms with Scots words and constructions represented as spoken. The writer in the West Indies today similarly has to decide whether he is going to use dialect consistently throughout his book, or just for parts of it, and whether he is going to adopt every feature of the dialect or just some features in any particular sentence. There is a range of options open to him. First, at one extreme he can simply make use of words and idioms with a distinctive West Indian meaning and flavour in what is otherwise more or less standard English. Or secondly, he can decide, say, to use dialect simply for the conversation of certain of his characters while using standing English for narrative prose and perhaps for the dialogue of other characters. Or, a third possibility, he can decide to have a go at being much more creative and reflect in his writing the wide spectrum of dialectal usage—from very broad vernacular to educated local usage—which is a feature of the verbal behaviour of many West Indians. In other words, if he cares to use it, he has at his command a tool which can create many different facets of West Indian life simply by shifting from one linguistic register to another. Finally he might try, as Vic Reid did (somewhat unsuccessfully I think) in *New Day* (Knopf, New York, 1949), to create for his purposes an amalgam between standard English and dialect and then use this throughout the book for all purposes. The modified standard English which Vic Reid developed had a very literary flavour and, for me at least, failed to carry conviction. But if he adopts my third possibility, the West Indian writer must face the fact that he is going to have to educate his readers to recognize the conventions which he is developing and which may accurately reflect West Indian life without necessarily registering immediately with West Indian readers. I would then look forward to a very healthy period when all West Indian writers interested in developing vernacular usage in literature in depth, for all registers, would be touring around West Indian schools and towns giving readings from their work just as Dickens did in England. This might be less comfortable than working for the BBC in London and talking only to other West Indian writers in exile, but it would be a way of ploughing back into the soil some of the nourishment which the writer draws from his own community and about which the West African novelist I referred to felt so guilty. And it would mean that West Indian writing had come of age, an indigenous literature in the indigenous language.

'Dialect in West Indian Literature', *Journal of Commonwealth Literature*, no. 7 (July 1969), pp. 1-7. (This article is based on a paper given at the Africa Centre, London, on 25 October 1967, the first of a series of seminars on 'Literature of Africa and the Caribbean'.)

GERALD MOORE

The Language of West Indian Poetry

... The most important of the discoveries made over the ... thirty
years [since the founding of the little magazine *Bim*] is that the West
Indies have languages of their own. Not curiosities for the linguist
and ethnologist to study, but living and developing languages which
have proved essential to the full revelation of West Indian life in
literature. Who can imagine the stories of Norma Hamilton or
Timothy Callender, the poems of Bongo Jerry or Audvil King,
written otherwise? What would Wilson Harris's *Palace* or *Oudin*
be without the deep, salty tang of Guyanese speech, which continually roots his poetic fantasies in social reality?

Such instances make it clear that the representation or creative
rehandling of a particular texture of West Indian sound (be it speech
or song) is not some sort of verbal decoration, more or less
dispensable, but the very material out of which the new literature
and drama are being wrought. Gone is the comic intrusion of the
Creole-speaker into the polite circle of the educated—strictly
comparable with the comic Cockney housemaid or manservant in
a pre-war West End play. How can what is indigenous and natural
to the vast body of people in a society be presented to them in a
comic or eccentric light, except by a kind of cultural confidence
trick? This trick, still played by many of those in authority in the
islands, takes in fewer people every time.

In West Indian drama we can already see the recognition of this
truth in works as early as Walcott's *The Sea at Dauphin* and *Ti
Jean and His Brothers*. In fiction it emerges in the contrast between
C. L. R. James's *Minty Alley* (1934) and Roger Mais's *The Hills
Were Joyful Together* (1953). Both were middle-class writers
reporting on a yardlife out of which they hadn't themselves sprung;
but the James novel, interesting and original as it is in its epoch,
presents the wrong kind of cultural centre by interposing its hero
(with a middle-class background like James's own) between the
reader and the yard. Mais suppresses this intervention, because
he offers us no figure in the yard with whom we can identify the
author himself. We are plunged straight into that life, and hence
participate imaginatively in it far more directly than if we were
encouraged to cling to the coat-tails of a character who is not really
of the yard himself, who experiences and interprets it for us, and

thus holds it at a distance from the reader. I don't want to exaggerate the notion of 'literary landmarks'. Mais's achievement had been anticipated in some ways by a book like *New Day*, and his own influence was not evenly or immediately fel, but it did significantly and permanently alter the map of Caribbean fiction.

The example of Mais and Reid, now some twenty years old, probably still stands somewhere in the emergence of writing like this, in Norma Hamilton's story 'Gan-Gan':

Dat stink-stink creature. Greeny and slimy-slimy creature. Rotten flesh. Worum. Evil. Tings dat hide wey fram sun an haffe live unda grung. Ah so di creature stan. How much nite now dat ole nasi ting run him dung wid lang fork fe juk him inna him batty-hole an wen i corna him an redy fi do di act an him a-bawl out 'Whai Oye! Whai Oye! Miss Marina. Miss Marina save me!' him wake up and dere is Miss Marina a-stare pon him friten, an cock a-crow an dawn a-bruk inna di sky and cole swet a-wash him an consciousness reach him, an him so glad to be out a arms reach fram dat creature.

By contrast it seems to have taken rather longer for West Indian poetry to develop a full consciousness of the living language situation which surrounds it. Although we might wish the Creole ballads of Louise Bennett and the best of the Calypso lyrics as poetry—indeed I believe we should—they were not perhaps fully apprehended as such by the audiences which first heard them, in the forties, fifties and even the sixties. Poetry was something else, something which appeared in little magazines, on BBC programmes, in rare anthologies and even rarer slim volumes. And it is poetry in these terms (though with the important added dimension of public readings) which has been transformed in the past few years; first by Brathwaite's trilogy, in which a sustained effort was made to identify the language bases (American and Caribbean folk-song, Akan drum rhythms, West Indian popular speech) on which a new poetry might be built; and more recently in the electric vitality of poets like Bongo Jerry:

MABRAK is righting the wrongs and brain-whitening—HOW?
Not just by washing out the straightening and wearing
        dashiki t'ing:
MOSTOFTHESTRAIGHTENINGISINTHETONGUE—so HOW?
Save the YOUNG
from the language that MEN teach,
the doctrine Pope preach
skin bleach.

How ELSE? . . . MAN must use MEN language to carry dis
        message:

SILENCE BABEL TONGUES; recall and
recollect BLACK SPEECH.

Notice how Jerry in this passage chucks the heavy stresses to and
fro within the line, demanding vocal agility and a quick eye in his
reader. This is a highly rhetorical poem, and it uses rhetoric in much
the same way as Brathwaite does in parts of his trilogy, though the
devices are broader and less meticulous. Whether this reflects the
influence Brathwaite has already exerted over his contemporaries or
a spontaneous and independent movement towards rhetoric in a
poetry where the lyrical mode has always prevailed hitherto, it
equally announces the kind of shift which has moved West Indian
poetry into new fields of apprehension and expression. Gone is
the polite tradition, afraid of letting out rude noises, and always
looking over its shoulder for approval *outside* the islands. Much
of the poetry in *Savacou 3-4* seems, rather, to exult in its freedom
from alien restraints. It is a poetry which restores the need for
immediate audience, even though it can be relished in solitary
reading also . . . .

With the exception of Mervyn Morris, who remains generally
faithful to the iambic pentameter and to a general stanzaic regu-
larity, most of the poets represented in *Breaklight* and in *Savacou
3-4* have felt the need to make formal changes which accord with
their new-found sense of assertion—assertion not merely *against*
the relics of the colonial order, but *for* the freedom to seek the bases
of their music where they will. And in the search for an appropriate
rhetoric, it is natural that poets like Bongo Jerry, Ras Dizzy and
Audvil King should make use of devices long practised by the
preachers, story-tellers and political leaders of the Caribbean;
devices which probably go back to the earliest cross-roads meetings
that prepared the great slave revolts of the seventeenth and
eighteenth centuries.

Look at the way Bruce St John uses the pulpit shout-and-response
technique to launch his poem on Stokeley Carmichael:

> Stokeley like he mad!
> *Da is true*
> He outah touch wid de West Indies.
> *Da is true*
> He ain't even discreet!
> *Da is true*
> He can't be pon we side.
> *Da is true*

or the use of a prosody very like that of Jamaican folk-song in
Richard Ho Lung's lullaby 'Mek Dream Tek Yu Life':

Ku pickney nurse mumma swell wid chil'
han pappa cut tinkin' toe walk ten mile;
see Abel ketch wata ah give to Cain.
So dutty tough but it ah rain.

Quiet, sweet pickney,
not cry yah,
sleep, hush, hush,
mek dream tek yuh life yah.

Even where the actual words and phrases used offer no dialect
features, the diction reflects a much greater awareness of what can
be done in English than was to be found in any poet writing in the
West Indies fifteen years ago. The chopped-up diction of Wayne
Brown's poem 'Red Hills' captures all the uneasiness behind the
self-satisfaction of the ... suburb above Kingston:

We arrive, sweating
from the long climb up,
loosen our ties and lapse

into grins. Red hillscar, red
nigger preserve,
our roses bloom whitely here.

It is interesting to compare this with the development of an older,
more established poet like Derek Walcott, whose early work was
stamped with the twin influences of the seventeenth century—
especially Marvell—and Dylan Thomas. The varied, complex
rhythm and difficult rhyme-scheme he employs in a mature poem
like 'Laventville' amount to a new poetic voice, free from that slight
air of provinciality which clung to a Caribbean poet, however
excellent, whose deep love of Enlgish poetry was so immediately
evident in everything he wrote. Let us take the opening lines of
'Laventville' (reprinted in *Breaklight*) for an example of this new
mastery:

It huddled there
steel tinkling its blue painted metal air,
tempered in violence, like Rio's favelas,

with snaking, perilous streets whose edges fell as
its episcopal turkey buzzards fall
from its miraculous hilltop

shrine,
down the impossible drop
to Belmont, Woodbrook, Maraval, St Clair

that shine
like pedlars' tin trinkets in the sun.
From a harsh . . .

The rhyme-pattern here (*a, a, b; b, c, d; e, d, a; e, f, g*) is only one of the devices which make this opening so effective. Note also the delayed drop on the word 'shrine' (we have been expecting the sense to break after 'hilltop'), which reinforces the sensation of vision swooping and falling over the slum roofs with the turkey-buzzards. Also the way in which the sharp, crackling sounds, 'steel tinkling', like hot metal snapping, return a few lines later in 'pedlars' tin trinkets'. The fact that stanzas 2 and 4 introduce two entirely new rhyme-sounds, whereas 1 and 3 offer either the reassurance of: *a, a* or the recapitulation of: *e, d, a* is only one of the devices which edge us forward into this poem with a certain feeling of uneasiness and exposure. To see how far Walcott had travelled by the time he wrote this poem, we need only compare it with an earlier piece of descriptive writing from a volume published in the early fifties;

These leaves lie just as well as was their custom
When we were boys, won by a Delphic Sibyl's
Statue at that green shuttered house;
Liquid the tongues of leaves, marble that pain,
To boys with huge cartoons sketched on the brain;
Soft with apologies, the leaves retract their vows.

That bungalow stood white against the skyline,
Greek as the marble, and in the studio . . .
A little man, short-sighted as a brush,
Bent over canvases, anxious like us to catch
The yellow sunlight in its old Vermeer.

In this poem, 'The Cracked Playground', the density of exotic reference which is typical of early Walcott (Delphic Sibyl, Greek marble, Vermeer) immediately situates it in terms of an audience which will appreciate and applaud this learned young colonial. It is the poet, with his 'shameful', 'audacious complexion', who looks like an intruder among this bric-à-brac of classical statues and literary relics. And this derivative relationship is equally reflected in the rather heavy, even movement of the pentameters. In these early poems Walcott depends on the metaphysical brilliance of his puns and conceits (e.g. 'retract their vows') to astonish the reader. He captures us by his exuberance, but is often wordy and showy. It is the more astonishing that another dozen years should bring the tragic authority of 'Laventville', or the cool yet bitter anger of 'The Gulf'.

I don't want to exaggerate the role of distinctively West Indian speech-patterns in the liberation of its poetry which the last few years have brought. Many of its most remarkable and original poets, such as Martin Carter, Dennis Scott and Faustin Charles, have not found it necessary to their purposes to use dialect words or phrases. The question of indigenous rhythms is more subtle and difficult to elicit. Many poets have moved towards a more flexible line-length, with a predominance of short lines and consequently stronger, swifter emphases. This verse from Knolly La Fortune's title-poem 'Breaklight' might serve as an example:

> We were the bolt
> the incredible willing jackpot,
> gunned down through the years.
> We were the black question-box.
> We were slotted into all available wars
> in foreign places.

Martin Carter, on the other hand, has made himself the master of a long-breathed, rather deliberate pace. Though he can use the whip-lash when necessary, some of his most memorable and beautiful works, like the famous 'Poems of Shape and Motion', owe a good deal of their effect to this characteristic pace, with attendant associations of night, introspection and solitary struggle:

> I walk slowly in the wind,
> remembering scorn and naked men in darkness
> and huts of iron standing on the earth
> like rusting prisons.

. . . The poetic map in the Caribbean, then, is full alike of variety and achievement. Many are the paths and means which its poets are finding towards a common liberation; various as the islands themselves, whose West Indianness is often only apparent when you look at them from far away. But beneath all the different choices of language, rhythm, line-length, musical stress and stanzaic form lies a general determination to use English in poetry as uninhibitedly as West Indians have long used it in speech and song. The poet is no longer a kind of putative Rhodes Scholar, learning his craft, his langugage and his references by way of 'English Literature'. In the words of Knolly La Fortune:

> We've seen through
> the writing on the wall.

There need no longer be any distracting debate about which language they 'ought' to use. From the formal classicism of

Mervyn Morris to the drum-beats of Bongo Jerry, these poets have equally something to write about, and their work is driven forward by an equal impulse to deliver it.

From 'Use Men Language', *Bim*, no. 57 (March 1974), pp. 69-76. This article was a review of *Savacou*, nos 3 and 4 (joint issue, December 1970-March 1971), and *Breaklight*, ed. Andrew Salkey (London, 1971).

MERVYN MORRIS

The Dialect Poetry of Louise Bennett

... I am told (I think on good authority) that Miss Bennett had been writing and speaking her poems for many years before she won general acceptance even as an entertainer. The Jamaican middle class was slow to acknowledge an interest in dialect which represented for most of them the speech-forms of a lower class from whom they wished to be distinguished. Our political and social history since about 1940 confirms the assertion that the Jamaican middle class have moved only very gradually towards an awareness of Jamaican identity; we have moved gradually from an unthinking acceptance of a British heritage to a more critical awareness of our origins and a greater willingness to acknowledge African elements of our past as part of our national personality. Dialect was, naturally, associated with our African past, because, basically, Jamaican dialect is English creolised by Africans and supplemented by some African words.

... Gradually, Louise Bennett won middle-class acceptance; though one may well wonder for what reasons. Is it not possible that many middle-class audiences laugh at dialect verse or drama for uncomfortable psychological reasons? My own observation suggests this. If one reads Louise Bennett to middle-class school children they are apt to laugh not only at wit and humour but at the language itself. The language which their maids and yardboys use is not yet accepted simply as one of our Jamaican ways of speech.

I write particularly of the middle-class because it is that class which must necessarily form at present the mass of a Jamaican reading-public, and which has so far been the bulk of our theatre audiences. It is for that class, mainly, that Louise Bennett has so far written and performed.

The middle class, then, came to accept Louise Bennett as an entertainer. . . .

... I do not believe that Louise Bennett is a considerable poet. But a poet, and, in her best work, a better poet than most other Jamaican writers she certainly is. She does not offer her readers any great insight into the nature of life or human experience, but she recreates human experience vividly, delightfully and intelligently. She is rarely pretentious—the most common fault in West

Indian poetry; she is not derived from other poets—she has her own interesting voice; and she is invariably sane.

... The form most often chosen by Miss Bennett is dramatic monologue. This is hardly surprising in a poet who often performs her work. She writes for the voice and the ear, and when her poems are expertly performed something more, movement, is added. The poem 'Candy Seller' should make these points clear.

Candy lady, candy mam?
Bizniz bad nowadays,
Lady wid de pretty lickle bwoy
Buy candy, gwan yuh ways!
Yu right fe draw de pickney han,
Koo pon him two nose hole,
Him y'ey dem a tare out like him want
Hickmatize me candy-bole.

Nice young man come here. Wat yuh want?
Pinda-cake? Wangla?
Ef yuh naw buy wey yuh stop fah!
Beg yuh move yuhself yaw sah.
Me noh ha notten dah gi way,
Gi de lady pass fe come,
Wey yuh noh go jine de air force?
Dem have plenty use fe bum.

Come lady buy nice candy mam?
Dem all is wat I meck.
Which kine yuh want mam, pepper-mint?
Tank yuh mam, Kiss me neck!
One no mo' farden bump she buy!
Wat a red kin 'oman mean!
Koo har foot eena de wedge-heel boot,
Dem favah submarine.

Ah weh she dah tun back fah? She
Musa like fe hear me mout
Gwan, all yuh shouldn' walk a day,
Yuh clothes fava black-out.
Me keahn pick up a big sinting
Like yuh so draw dat blank.
Afta me noh deh a war, me naw
Colleck no German tank.

Cho—go-way—Come here nice white man
Don't pass me by soh sah!
See me beggin' by de roadside.
Come buy a nice wangla.
W'en wite people go fe ugly
Massa dem ugly sah.

Koo ow dat de man face heng dung
Lacka w'en jackass feel bad.

Me dah liff up now yaw Dinah,
Lacka ow dem lock up store
An' everybody dah go home,
Me naw go sell much more.
Me wi' cry out as me go along,
Me mighta get a brake—
By peppermint—till later awn
Me gawn—Fresh pindacake.

The Candy-Seller is addressing a number of different people in
a number of different tones of voice. Her wheedling to prospective
customers plays off against her cursing of them as they pass on,
and the last stanza clearly says that she is about to move on, her less
personal cries ('Buy peppermint', 'Fresh pindacake') contrasting
with her earlier invitations ('Come lady buy nice candy mam?').
As in a Browning monologue, the entire dramatic situation is made
clear without the direct intervention of the author. The whole poem
convinces; it has a vitality that seems perfectly to match the
imagined context. The images focus on war because the poem was
written in wartime and it was perfectly natural that the first abuse
that came to mind should relate to war. If anyone doubts the
precise suitability of the images—wedge-heel boot like submarine,
clothes like black-out, and so on—he should be disarmed by the
dramatic context. This could all well be said by a candy-seller in
this situation. Rhythm and rhyme are used effortlessly, the pauses
coming where the dramatic sense demands them. There is no
constriction, no monotony. The poem has the oneness, the wholeness, of a completely realized experience. What more does literary
taste ask for?

Several other of Louise Bennett's dramatic monologues could
survive detailed examination: for example, 'Street Boy', in which
a youngster, held by a policeman for swearing, pleads with passers-
by to beg for him, appeals to the policeman's memory of his own
young days, thanks him extravagantly when he lets him go, and
then, once out of reach, gloats: 'Ah get weh doah, yuh brut!'
'Parting', where the situation is a platform farewell, and 'South
Parade Pedlar' are other outstanding monologues of this type.

Sometimes the situation is presented through the poet as story-
teller rather than directly through characters. A good example of
this is 'Dry Foot Bwoy', in which the affected speech of a boy just
home from England is dramatically contrasted with the story-
teller's Jamaican dialect:

Me gi a joke, de gal dem laugh
But hear de bwoy, 'Ha-haw!

I'm sure you got that bally-dash
Out of the cinema!'

Same time me las' me tempa, an
Me halla, 'Bwoy kir out!
No chat to me wid no hot pittata
Eena yuh mout!'

In some of her poems Louise Bennett is not just a story-teller
but is herself the central character. 'Television' is an example of
this. There she communicates the excitement of the occasion:

Red light start flash, de place start get
Quiet and quieta.
Dem put me fe tan up fronten
Bans a big camera!

One man start ask me question
Bout folksong and all dem ting,
One guitar start fe rythm up,
An den me start fe sing.

Me never even nervous an me
Never even shy,
Me tan up brazen like pus bruck
Coc'nut eena me yeye!

It was just like movin' pictures
Me was jus like movies queen
Wid camera dah flash pon screen.

An as fe all me frien dem! Po
Miss Manda feeling gran.
She dah boas bout how her choky-bead
Ac' pon television.

Perhaps there is a trace of falsity here: one is not entirely convinced
of the ordinariness of this performer. The milieu is wrong. She can
convince us that she is a peasant or a maid or a market-woman or
a street-boy, but somehow the television studio reminds us too
forcibly that Miss Bennett is a trained performer; dialect seems
imposed on the situation.
   . . . I have claimed that Louise Bennett is a very sane poet and
that she has generosity of spirit. She is always attacking pretension
by laugher, and sometimes by hard logic. An example of logic
would be 'Back to Africa' in which an argument is ruthlessly
followed through:

Back to Africa Miss Matty?
Yuh no know wa yuh dah sey?

Yuh haffe come from some weh fus,
Before yuh go back deh.

Me know sey dat yuh great great great
Granma was African,
But Matty, doan yuh great great great
Grampa was Englishman?

Den yuh great gran mada fada
By yuh fada side was Jew!
And yuh grampa by yu mada side
Was Frenchie parley-vous!

But de balance a yuh family
Yuh ole generation
Oonoo all bawn dung a Bun grung,
Oonoo all is Jamaican!

Den is weh yuh gwine Miss Matty?
Oh, you view de countenance
An betweens yuh and de Africans
Is a great resemblance!

Ascorden to dat, all dem blue-eye
Wite American,
Wa great granpa was Englishman
Mus go back a Englan!

Wat a debil of a bump-an-bore,
Rig-jig an palam-pam!
Ef de ole world' start fe go back
Weh dem great granpa come from!

Ef a hard time yuh dah run from,
Tek yuh chance, but Matty, do
Sure a weh yuh come from so yuh got
Someweh fe come-back to!

Go a foreign, seek yuh fortune,
But no tell nobody sey
Yuh dah go fe seek yuh homelan
For a right deh so yuh deh!

It takes a shape very eighteenth-century in its careful balance, the balance helping to point the strictly logical operation of a keen intelligence. Louise Bennett's sanity takes her straight to a fact that too many intellectuals, evidently, find too simple for their acceptance: the central fact of our identity: that we are Jamaicans because Jamaica is where we come from.

Miss Bennett's irony is sometimes easy and cheap; but it is also

sometimes important and illuminating. In her poem 'Independence'
she sets our national aspirations in perspective:

> She hope dem caution worl-map
> Fe stop draw Jamaica small
> For de lickle speck can't show
> We Independantniss at all!

Often the pretensions attacked are minor or topical pretensions,
but not always. Look for example at 'Po' Ting' in which a
common, and no doubt eternal, human pretension is ridiculed,
unwillingness to face the fact of age:

> Po' Miss Mattie, Po' Miss Mattie!
> Ah pity de po' soul,
> Me haffe goh bruck it genkly
> Soh tell her sey she ole.
>
> Me meet her pon de tram one night
> An' mek me tell yuh trut',
> De way she dress, she tryin' hard
> Fe bring back days of yout'.
>
> But Missis powda ongle mek
> De po' ting 'kin more yella,
> An' rouge an' lip-stick meck de wrinkle
> Dem tan up fe de betta.
>
> Before she kip herself quiet,
> An' meck by-gones goh by,
> As she turn roun' an' se' me soh,
> De po' soul cut har y'eye.
>
> Yuh know how she look widdad up,
> An' shapeless aready?
> Well lawd wen har y'eye kin come dung
> She fava dead smaddy.
>
> She start fe smile, but missis she
> Was eena de same place,
> For wen she laugh it look like she
> Dah mek up monkey face.
>
> Ah go fe laugh out afta har,
> But ah nevah bada,
> For ah consider sey she ole
> Enough fe tun me mada.
>
> So wen she jump off like she young
> An' start fe walk an' swing,
> Ah ongle shake me head an' sigh
> An' say to meself 'Po' ting.'

There is a touch of pathos in that last stanza, I feel. The comic treatment here is more acceptable, and I think more delicate, than Gilbert's sometimes cruel laughter at women growing old:

> She may very well pass for forty-three
> In the dusk, with a light behind her.

There is a good deal of simple plain fun in Louise Bennett. Sometimes it is fun in the situation, as in, say, 'De Bathsuit And De Cow', an excellent little dialect ballad. Sometimes the fun is an intoxication with language which she manipulates or invents with infectious delight:

> Riah tun pon Butcha Jones who noted
> Fe sell all scrapses meat
> An sey 'Thou shalt not give thy neighbours
> Floolooloops to eat!'

Or, as in 'Cuss Cuss':

> Me sorry fe de man yuh get
> De po ting hooden nyam
> When yuh ackebus him saltfish
> An bwilivous him yam.

It is not my main purpose in this essay to demonstrate Miss Bennett's weaknesses, but it may be well to mention some of her problems or faults and to attempt to define her limitations.

I think her most central difficulty is choice of subject. Many of her poems are a sort of comic-verse-journalism; she is quick to tackle the topical; which is only natural, as she published her early and some of her later poems in newspapers. One willingly says good-bye to numerous poems about new Governors, new pantomimes, Paul Robeson's visit, a Test match victory, and so on, where interest has not survived the topicality of the subject. As in the same periods as her very topical poems she wrote others of more lasting interest, we can hardly complain: we can only regret that so much of the journalism has been published in book form. It would be a service to her readers if Miss Bennett would present a Collected Poems, dropping all the ephemera and choosing the best of the others. (Different criteria were adopted by Miss Bennett and Mr Rex Nettleford in selecting poems for *Jamaica Labrish* (Jamaica, Sangster's, 1966).)

Miss Bennett is sometimes false to her medium. I have been careful not to parade these falsities, but even in the poems I have quoted some may be found. For example, in 'Back to Africa' the stanza:

Den is weh yu gwine Miss Matty?
Oh, you view de countenance,
An between yuh and de Africans
Is a great resemblance!

'Countenance' is doubtful for the dialect level of the rest of the
poem, and certainly 'resemblance' (for the rhyme) cannot pass:
at that level of dialect, we favour Africans, surely, we don't
resemble them.

To anybody who thinks that a lively metrical sense and some
wit are sufficient equipment for writing dialect verse like Miss
Bennett's, I suggest he make the attempt. He will find, as Miss
Bennett herself has found, that dialect has to be felt, like any other
poetic language.

To trace Louise Bennett's development is interesting. She
develops, I think, from the high-spirited monologuist to a more
purposeful thinker writing in dialect: it is not for nothing that the
mature irony of 'Independence' or the logic of 'Back to Africa'
are recent, and the best dramatic monologues are early. Or,
compare the tone of 'Gay Paree' (an earlyish poem in which there
is a childlike peasant delight in the strangeness of French) with the
tone of 'Touris' (much later, in which the poet sees herself
ironically, with a certain sophistication).

Den me sey me want fe learn it to,
Me haffe buckle dung,
Screw up me mout and roll me y'eye
An foreign up me tongue.

An hear me now dah parley-vous
Dah tell yuh mon cheree
What a joli-joli bon-bon time
Me spen in Gay Paree
                    ('Gay Paree')

Missis, you would a dead wid laugh
Fe hear me touris voice!
Fe hear how me a pop big words
An gwan like say me nice!

When me listen to sweet music
Me say 'Charming melody.'
When me se some pretty sights me say
'Delightful scenery.'

We walk into de bigges' store
Dilly-dally all bout',
Touch up de mos expensive tings
Den say 'tanks' an walk out.
                    ('Touris')

In between these two stages of development Miss Bennett spent some years in England; when she returned she wrote what I consider some of her worst pieces. The dialect was forced and untrue:

> So May, me dear, now dat yuh hear
> All bout how me dah drive
> No fret no more for now yuh sure
> You darlin frien mus trive.

'Trive'! She made some metrical experiments she would have done well to keep out of print. A fair example is the internal jingle of 'Pedestrian Crossin'', a jingle which seems to have no function. The rapidity of her normal stanza form is lost, and, it seems, nothing is gained:

> Now me chance come at last,
> As dem cros ah gwine pass,
> Ah mus beat dah ole-oman to dis,
> By de hook or de crook—
> Lawd one police a look!
> 'Pass on lady, your right of way, Miss.'

It would seem that the dialect (or Louise Bennett using it) cannot cope with a rocking rhythm such as this.

Living in Jamaica again, Miss Bennett seemed to grow into dialect again, though she never regained her early innocent vitality. I think that accounts for the greater pervasiveness of acute intelligence in the later poems and the decreasing inclination to rumbustious dramatic monologue. Miss Bennett's own development seems to show that her use of dialect is involved with real feeling, as is any poet's use of language.

A weakness, particularly in the early poems, is for direct and unsubtle moralising. In the later poems any sentimentality or tendency to moralise is usually redeemed by irony or wit. It is instructive to compare her poem 'Homesickness' with a rather well-known poem which scarcely deserves its frequent quotation. In 'Homesickness' Miss Bennett gives a sentimental list of things she misses while in England; the list does name things we can recognise as part of a real Jamaica: bullas, sugar and water, dumplings; but is nevertheless a sentimental selection in its total effect. But the last three stanzas run:

> For me long fe see a bankra basket
> An a hampa load,
> A number-leven, beafy, blacky,
> Hairy mango pon de road!

An me mout top start fe wata
Me mout corner start fe foam,
A dose a hungry buckle hole me
An me wan fe go back home.

Go back home to me Jamaica
To me fambly! To me wa?
Lawd ha masse, me fegot,
All a me fambly over yah!

Easy as that final irony is, it redeems the poem. It gives a guarantee that there is a mind alive behind it all. The lush sentimentality of H. D. Carberry's 'I Shall Remember' fares badly in a comparison with 'Homesickness' (which is hardly one of Louise Bennett's finer poems).

Louise Bennett's use of Jamaican dialect is not, of course, the only literary use there is. Our Jamaican folk songs, for example, are a rich store, and they seem to suggest (what one might reasonably have guessed even without their evidence) that our dialect can be used for other effects than Miss Bennett has so far attempted. Let us examine one song briefly:

Dis long time gal me never see you
Come meck me hol' you han'
Dis long time gal me never see you
Come meck me hol' you han'.

Peel head John Crow
Si' dung pon tree top
Pick off de blossom
Meck me hol' you han' gal
Come meck me hol' you han'.

Here there is a deeper, more obviously 'poetic' symbolism than Miss Bennett ever attempts. The John Crow picking the blossoms I take to be an image of death encroaching on beautiful promising young life; and this clearly deepens the significance of

Dis long time gal me never see you
Come meck me hol' you han'.

The song becomes more than just another love-song; it is deeply involved with time and mortality.

'Carry Me Ackee' does not have this sort of deepening, but its poignancy seems outside the range of what Miss Bennett tries.

All me pickney dem a linga linga
Fe wey dem Mumma no bring.

It is a very sad song, quite as sad as the Frats Quintet sing it on their record.

Evan Jones's 'Banana Man' uses a dialect level different from Louise Bennett's. It is nearer standard English. This poem achieves a power beyond Louise Bennett's published range; the Banana Man seems to stand partly as a symbol of strength, freedom, self respect.

> I'm a strong man, a proud man, an' I'm free,
> Free as these mountains, free as dis sea.

The last poem I want to mention is of a different kind. It is Dennis Scott's 'My Uncle Time', a consummate poem:

> Uncle Time is a ole, ole man . . .
> All year long 'im wash 'im foot in de sea,
> long, lazy years on de wet san'
> and shake de coconut tree
> dem quiet-like wid 'im sea-win' laughter,
> scraping away de lan' . . .
>
> Uncle Time is a spider-man, cunning an' cool,
> him tell yu': watch de hill an' you se me,
> Huh! Fe yu' yi no quick enough fe si
> how 'im move like mongoose; man, yu' t'ink 'im fool?
> Me Uncle Time smile black as sorrow;
> 'im voice is sof' as bamboo leaf
> but Lawd, me Uncle cruel.
> When 'im play in de street
> wid yu' woman—watch 'im! By tomorrow
> she dry as cane-fire, bitter as cassava; an' when 'im
>   teach yu son, long after
> yu' walk wid stranger, an' yu' bread is grief.
> Watch how 'im spin web rou' yu' house, an' creep
> inside; an' when 'im touch yu', weep.

Here we have a poet using dialect, as Walcott does in 'Poopa da' was a fête', for artistic purposes that don't seem natural to dialect at all. The poem has been thought, so to speak, in standard English. Louise Bennett uses dialect more or less as we can believe the normal speakers of dialect might use it, if they were skilled enough; Walcott and Scott borrow dialect for the literary middle class. The image 'smile black as sorrow' is too abstract for the eminently concrete medium of dialect. It must be said, however, that this poem has a careful exquisite beauty that I cannot claim for anything in Louise Bennett.

Louise Bennett, then, is a poet of serious merit, although like all poets, she has her limitations. Like most poets she is, I have tried to show, developing. And she is so much more rewarding a poet than many to whom we in Jamaica give the name, that it seems reasonable to expect more of those who claim an interest in poetry to give her more attention. She is sane; throughout, her poems imply that sound common sense and generous love and under-standing of people are worthwhile assets. Jamaican dialect is, of course, limiting (in more senses than one); but within its limitations Louise Bennett works well. Hers is a precious talent . . . .

'On Reading Louise Bennett, Seriously', *Jamaica Journal*, vol. 1 (December 1967), pp. 69-74. (This essay was written in 1963 and awarded first prize in the 1963 Jamaica Festival essay competition.)

JOHN FIGUEROA

Derek Walcott's 'Poopa, Da' Was a Fête!' and Evan Jones's 'Lament of the Banana Man'

I should like to consider 'The Lament of the Banana Man' by Evan Jones . . . and 'Tales of the Islands, Chap. VI' by Derek Walcott . . . in connection with the way in which a poet might use the West Indian language situation.

These two poems are clearly both of high quality, but they do use the West Indian language continuum in quite differing ways. In a moment we will examine them from that point of view. At present let us note that they both use the device, among others, of antithesis, of polarity, in which the feeling and the imagery run back and forth between two apparently contrary or contradictory moments:

> But that was long before this jump and jive

where 'that' refers to the 'fête'; while 'fête' stands against:

> the heart
> Of a young child was torn from it alive
> By two practitioners of native art.

'Native art' stands against 'one of them Oxbridge guys' and

> Each
> Generation has its *angst*, but we has none

is a sort of central antithesis standing against everything else in the poem, generating glorious ambiguity and irony within itself. Note the force of 'we has none'—but also throwing off sparks, inducing current to 'jump the gap' between itself and so many things in the poem including the 'two tests up the beach', free rum, free whisky, eating and drinking.

Likewise in the Jones poem there are both irony—perhaps of a gentler kind—and a meaningful juxtaposition of many moments:

> Gal, I'm tellin' you, I'm tired fo' true
> Tired of Englan', tired o' you

against:

> But I can' go back to Jamaica now.

and

> My yoke is easy, my burden is light.

against the rest of the poem.

There is a further polarity within that statement itself because the reader recognises that it is a quotation from the Bible, but is not sure whether the 'Banana Man' does; further, it is by far the most 'standard' English line of the poem. Finally, against everything else:

> But I'd want to die there, anyhow.

All this is true, but as far as the relationship of the poet to his medium is concerned, Jones tends to reproduce (excellently), Walcott to *use*, the local language. Jones's 'dialect' is formalised and accurate enough to *place* the person speaking, to lend verisimilitude (and pathos) to the fictional situation. A certain kind of person is speaking and that certain kind of person necessarily uses a certain kind of language if what he says is to appear to be really *his*. But the real antitheses are not between styles and registers of language, but between the overt and latent consciousness, and content, of the Banana Man's dream:

> Tired of Englan', tired o' you

versus

> But I can' go back to Jamaica now;

and

> You won' catch me bawling' any homesick tears
> If I don' see Jamaica for a t'ousand years.

versus

> Tired of Englan' tired o' you

versus

> I can't go back to Jamaica now—
> But I'd want to die there, anyhow.

In respect of the language situation, of the rich and confused West Indian heritage of English and Creole, Jones in this poem is a reproducer rather than an exploiter. The only real *use* which he makes of the *levels* of language which are present in the Creole situation is to be found in the appearance of

My yoke is easy, my burden is light

where the 'upward' movement into 'standard' language (and into the overtones of the Bible) has certain analogies with the Walcott 'downward' movement so well sounded in the second 'has' in

Each
Generation has its *angst*, but we has none.

Walcott *uses* the language situation: with him it is not a matter of verisimilitude, or local colour, but of essential and rich meaning which he conveys through, and by, the full resources of the West Indian language continuum, with its various levels. It is, be it noted, in the eighth line of the sonnet—at the point where by *tradition* there is expected to be a 'turn', a twist, a certain newness —that Walcott uses 'has' in the way just referred to.

The sonnet starts with the Creole intonation, Creole phonology, Creole structure:

Poopa, da' was a fête! I mean it had
Free rum free whisky and some fellars beating
Pan from one of them band in Trinidad
And everywhere you turn was people eating
And drinking and don't name me but I think
They catch his wife with two tests up the beach.*

and then we move through *'angst'* (preceded by the sonority of 'each/Generation has . . .') to the out of place (and therefore, in the context of the poem, superbly *in place*) Creole usage of 'has' for 'have'; and finally to the much more 'standard' final four lines:

And it was round this part once that the heart
Of a young child was torn from it alive
By two practitioners of native art,
But that was long before this jump and jive.

Note that the last line, colloquial in effect, and with effect, is colloquial not in the terms of Creole, but of slightly slangy English:

---

*Contrast all of this section of the sonnet with Jones's 'My yoke is easy, my burden is light'.

. . . before this jump and jive.

One is not trying to set up invidious comparisons, with regard to quality, between Jones and Walcott in these poems; one is merely trying to show that Walcott is here an innovator. He is not only reproducing 'the dialect' as the 'true' speech of a certain person; he is also embodying and expressing through the very heterogeneity of our language situation a certain basic relationship (in the West Indies) between 'fête' and *angst*; between 'Oxbridge guys' and 'native art'; between two kinds of celebration. And he does this partly by his masterly use of the Creole base which breaks through all the Oxbridge and the existentialist 'philosophy' in the shape of 'we has none'.

In the space of one sonnet he significantly uses the variety of speech and language which exists in the Creole situation—he uses this variety to do what could not be done in an homogeneous speech community. In other words he turns a situation often considered to be confusing and somehow 'backward' entirely to his, and our, advantage.

The statement of Robert Graves that Walcott 'handles English with a closer understanding of its inner magic than most (if not all) of his English-born contemporaries' is not at all unrelated to the fact that Walcott comes from a community in which there is a crude form of speech and it is *accepted*. The significance of a person like Walcott and his approach to language, is that situations which are often labelled 'disadvantageous' are only so when shamefully run from and disowned, rather than creatively used. A community with a wide spectrum of language varieties should be the richer, not the poorer, by that fact. The works of Evan Jones, of Dennis Scott, of Louise Bennett, of Edward Brathwaite, of Andrew Salkey, all point to this truth. But Walcott best, perhaps, exemplifies it.

His use of language should, for this reason, especially speak to all those who have grown up using a 'dialectal' form of a standard language—but of course Walcott has a command of the whole continuum, not just of one end of it.

Appendix ('Our Complex Language Situation') to *Caribbean Voices*, vol. 2 (London: Evans Bros, 1970), pp. 225-8.

GORDON ROHLEHR

Samuel Selvon and the Language of the People

... In *A Brighter Sun* (London, 1952) Selvon examines the rapid semi-urbanisation of the village of Barataria, during the years of the Second World War, and the corresponding emergence of the Indian peasant in a Creolised culture. This he does by tracing a gradual expansion of the consciousness of Tiger, the central figure of the novel, and by understanding that the movement from a 'folk' to a 'semi-urban' situation is paralleled by subtle shifts in language.

Ramlal, an old Indian peasant, is one of the last group of indentured labourers whose first language is Hindi, and whose Creole is cryptic, and entirely functional. Here, for example, he maps out Tiger's entire destiny in three curt sentences:

> You gettam house which side Barataria, gettam land, cow—well, you go live dat side. Haveam plenty boy chile—girl chile no good, only bring trouble on yuh head. Yuh live dat side, plantam garden, live good.

Tiger's speech oscillates between an early syntax pretty close to his father's, Ramlal's and Sookdeo's, to the free-flowing articulacy in Trinidad dialect, characteristic of the urban Creole, the linguistic continuum paralleling the socio-cultural one.[1] Early in the book, in one of his many statements about manhood, Tiger says: 'To my wife I man when I sleep with she. To *bap* I man if drink rum. But to me I no man yet.'

This is not quite the syntax of the fully urbanised Creole. Tiger senses that part of the problem of adjusting to the changes in his society and status, and also of his quest for significance, is one of creating a language supple enough to deal with the growing complexities which accompany his loss of rural innocence. He understands this task in the traditional fashion of Creole Trinidad. Painfully learning to read, he creates a language of polysyllabic words culled from a dictionary, by means of whose impressive sound he seeks to assert the manhood which he believes is eluding him all the time. This make-shift language, analogous to the

'signifying' of American Negroes, has been ritualised by the
Carnival masqueraders in Trinidad called the Midnight Robbers.[2]

Tiger senses, or is made to feel by the ridicule he occasions,
that 'robber talk' is a false, or at least an inadequate language in
which to conduct his quest for manhood, and one of the barriers
towards self-liberation is overcome when he rejects his fabricated
speech for one which genuinely expresses how he feels. In a
splendid scene towards the end of the book, Tiger has occasion to
reprimand two doctors, a Negro and an Indian, both of whom
refused to come out on a rainy night to attend to his wife:

> I is a Trinidadian like yourself, and it was a white man who had
> to come to poor Tiger hut to see he wife, while you and that
> other nasty coolie man who say he is a doctor too didn't want
> to come.

The passage is interesting for a number of reasons. Firstly, Tiger
himself through his very West Indian belief that manhood lies in
beating his woman, has brought on his wife's illness after a particularly brutal and wrong-headed beating. He thus exposes himself
to the equally brutal callousness of the Trinidadian doctors.
Secondly, the phrase 'nasty coolie man', a colonial epithet which
has its parallel in phrases such as 'black-and-ugly' or 'stupid ole
nigger', shows the keenness of Selvon's ear and the completeness of
his control. It is precisely the phrase which a Negro might have used
in abusing an Indian. Hence an ironic twist is given to the phrase
'I is a Trinidadian like yourself'. It means that the Creolisation
process is partly an exercise in colonial self-contempt, even when
one is in the act of claiming one's rights as a full citizen.

The complexities of the Creolisation process were reflected in
the insistent theme of race and racism, in the calypsoes of the
forties, the period which Selvon is covering in *A Brighter Sun*.
On the one hand, there were a few people who viewed these
calypsoes as a sign of emerging nationhood. The politician Albert
Gomes was one of these. In one of several articles on the Calypso,
he wrote:

> While so much of us are oblivious of the fact, the calypso singer
> has begun to announce in his songs that our ethnic 'potpourrie'
> is a reality, and that its many pots have begun to pour one into
> the other. The welding of our polyglot community is taking
> place before our eyes in the 'tents' and the weddings of our
> culture are being celebrated right there.
>
> Indian and Chinese tunes are being woven into the fabric of
> our calypso, and as though to give formal acceptance to yet
> another fact that should be obvious, the jumping jive, the

samba, the conga and the rhumba are becoming part of the music of the tent.[3]

More recently, Albert Gomes, who has for many years been residing in England, seems to have revised this simplistic reduction of the Creolisation process to a fairly pleasant melting-pot experience. He sees himself as having been defeated by the 'maze of colour' and racial prejudice which, he now says, had grown more pronounced from the late thirties to the late fifties—from Uriah Butler of 1937 to Eric Williams of 1956.[4] At least the later assessment, whatever it omits in its discussion of Gomes's political demise, does not simplify the complexities of the Creolisation process.

Neither did the calypsonians of the forties, whose songs reflected, if they did not analyse, the frequent harshness of the process of acculturation. Calypsonians mocked at Indians, Chinese, Baptists, Barbadians; sang about lack of morals in white society; castigated Trinidad women for going out with American soldiers, even when, at times, they themselves were prepared to exist off the earnings of such women. In other words, calypsonians, the extremest products of the process of urbanisation, provided a sounding board by which all 'intruders' on the urban scene were placed. Licensed eccentrics themselves, they mocked at what they saw as the eccentricity of others. The mockery which took the form of 'picong', a kind of wit based on caricature, reductive sarcasm and at times good humour, was a *rite de passage*, which ensured that creolisation took place on the basis approved by the urban-Creoles themselves.

Hence, reference to Indians and Chinese tended to be reductive, to stress existing stereotypes. Hindi and 'Indian' melodies were mocked in the Calypso. For the Indian peasant, the processes of urbanisation and acculturation tended to merge. Calypsonians noted this with what seems to have been scorn. Killer, for example, a calypsonian of the forties, noted the process of acculturation in Indians who rejected their Indian names:

> What's wrong with these Indian people
> As though their intention is for trouble
> Long ago you'd meet an Indian by the road
> With his capra waiting to take people load
> But I notice there is no Indian again
> Since the women and them taking Creole name
> Long ago was Sumintra, Ramnaliwia,
> Bullbasia and Oosankilia,
> But now is Emily, Jean and Dinah
> And Doris and Dorothy.

The prostitution unleashed on entire villages during the Yankee occupation of Trinidad during the war, is noted with the usual cynicism. The calypsonian seems to envy the Indian women even their success as good time girls. In this field also the Indian was regarded then as an outsider:

> Long ago you hadn't a chance
> To meet an Indian girl in a dance
> But nowadays it is big confusion
> Big fighting in the road for their Yankee man
> And you see them in the market, they ain't making joke
> Pushing down nigger people to buy their pork
> And you see them in the dances in Port-of-Spain
> They wouldn't watch if you call an Indian name.

What one notes here is that the calypsonian is seeing Port-of-Spain as the centre of his activities, and regarding the Indian as a new arrival on the scene, who must be levelled. What is also interesting is that in mocking at the Indian, the calypsonian reveals his own self-contempt or lack of a self-image. While he notes the loss of name and customs among Indians in the city, he can still use the insulting epithet to refer to his own people, the 'nigger people'. This is exactly what is happening to Selvon's Tiger in *A Brighter Sun*. Several calypsoes can be used as examples of what was happening during the forties as regards Creolisation and race relations. Only one more will be cited. In 'Moonia', sung by the Mighty Dictator, a courtship between an Indian girl and a Creole (Negro) is the theme:

> Well, I was in love with an Indian
> I was born in Jerningham Junction
> I couldn't see
> Eye to eye with her family
> But she said, 'Me lika de kessing
> And de Kirwal [creole] hugging and squeezing'
> The courtship stall
> When her mother jump up and bawl . . .
> . . . 'Moonia, Moonia,
> Bap na like am Kirwal, Moonia . . .'

The mother raises valid objections, by pointing out that the Indian peasant Ramlogan can offer cattle, a house and a reasonable match, while the Creole (urban and most probably unemployed) offers nothing:

> Well, de mother jump and mention
> 'This is the height of provacation
> How baytẹe

> Coulda likeam dat Kirwali?'
> She say, 'You know, Ramlogan house got cattle
> The Kirwal can't gie am nutten'
> Baytee a cry, 'Kirwal plantam me garden, Mai'.

And the father raises the final objection, with which the Creole seems half to agree. The Negro, he says, can offer only sexuality, which his 'fast' daughter seems to value above all things:

> Arguing with her mother
> Her father jump in the picture
> Before my eyes
> He started to criticise
> This time he said, 'What matter baytee?
> That Kirwal . . .
> You got um speed,
> So you likeam dat nigger breed.'

This transcription of the calypso is not word perfect. There are several places where the recording is unclear, and others where the calypsonian mocks at Indian accent and 'Hindi', the dotted line being one of them. What is clear is the unillusion of the calypsonian about the process of racial contact. Selvon, like the calypsonian, was clear about the implications of Tiger's 'advance' from 'Indian' to 'citizen'. He retains fair detachment throughout the story, but would have shared Tiger's rejection of the false values of the Port-of-Spain city slickers. On the other hand, he does not reject the process of Creolisation *per se*, as does, for example, V. S. Naipaul's Ralph Kripalsingh, anti-hero of *The Mimic Men*, who sees Creolisation as holding the horror of miscegenation, as violation of Aryan purity. Selvon seems to view history and change as things which one must accept. In so far as Tiger does arrive at a solution for his existential problems it is this:

> You don't start over things in life. . . . You just have to go on from where you stop. It not as if you born all over again. Is the same life. . . .

Much has been made of the calypso, mainly because in the calypso one has a permanent record not only of the passing phases of humour in Trinidad, but of how language was spoken, of the spirit of 'ole talk', 'picong', 'mamaguy', abuse, from decade to decade. Selvon, in his stories about Port-of-Spain urban/Creole life, is relating to the same tradition of style and rhetoric which produced calypsonians like the legendary Spoiler, Wonder, Panther, Melody, Lion, Tiger, Invader, Atilla, Kitchener, Beginner and Dictator, all figures of the forties.

These artists had a special language which involved heightening of the mundane and humdrum into melodrama, or 'bacchanal' as it is normally called. Gesture and mime reinforced speech. The language of the city was also the language of the small-time confidence trickster, the Brer Anansi figure who so often appears in Selvon's fiction, and whose method is to spin words fast enough to ensnare his victim, or, in the case of the calypsonian, to 'captivate' his audience.

Selvon brilliantly captures the language of the Port-of-Spain ole talk [gossip] in this passage about taxi-drivers, which appears in *A Brighter Sun*. The breathless prose, quicksilver fluidity of the passage can be compared with an excellent short story by Daniel Samaroo Joseph, called 'Taxi Mister',[5] or calypsoes such as Lord Melody's 'Peddlars', or Panther's 'Taxi-Drivers':

> Boy, dese taximen does have tings their own way too much. Some of dem does tell you dey leaving right away, and wen yuh get in de car, is because dey making round all Charlotte Street for more passengers, and wat yuh cud do? Nothing, because. yuh in de car already. As for weh dey going down South! Boy, dat is trouble self. All dem touts by de railway station, from de time dey see yuh wid a grip in yuh hand, dey start hustling. 'South, Mister?' 'Yuh going South? Look ah nice car here—it have radio—Leaving right away. South Direct. An dis time, de smart driver have 'bout three tout sitting down quiet as if dey is passengers.

To clinch the point about Selvon's relation to an oral tradition of the streets, the urban 'lime', the Calypso (Selvon has a story called 'Calypsonian'), I'll just quote bits of Panther's 'Taxi-Drivers':

> You may be standing on any pavement
> Asking someone questions on the government
> All you see is taxis in a line
> And all you do is answering questions all the time . . .
>
>   CHORUS
> An is PeeeeP . . . One to go
> You shake your head, you tell them no
> Braaw . . . they blow again
> You shake your head you tell them no again
> And is, San Juan, Tunapuna, Arima, Sangre Grande . . . Madam, you going? I am de fellar who give you a lift in Toco last week . . . You can't remember me?
> And they pointing their finger all over the place
> Somebody have a right to spit in their face.

This happen to me up by Globe Theatre
Ole talking, meself and the Tiger
Tell you the truth I didn't want no taxi,
In long and in short I was going to matinee
Man, up comes a taxi driver
'Panther! You going Point Cumana?'
'Whe a going deh for? I ain't got no fishing boat'
He take a knife and nearly cut way me throat
And is . . . Peeep, etc.

He say, 'Panther, you're a old calypsonian I know a long time. You
mean to say when I want to go to Carenage you won't go wid me?
Whe is it at all? anywhere you going ah carrying you, Diego Martin,
Four Road, Tamana Bucco Point, Uphill . . . any way at all . . .'

Ah say, 'You could be going down to Devil's Bay
Leave me here! I ain't going no way.'

The sections in prose are spoken rapidly in the tones of the
hustler above the rhythm of the calypso. The calypsonian regards
the taxi-man as yet another smart man, who is using language
against the citizen, rather than one who is trying to make a living.
The language, an abstract from the language of the streets, is little
different from Selvon's dramatic prose. Both Selvon and Panther
relate to an oral tradition, but in this case it is a different tradition
from that of the Trinidad folk-song, say, having grown out of
the process of acculturation in the town.

Since the epithet 'folk' has been most insistently applied to the
work of Selvon, one feels justified in spending the most time on
it, to point out its variety and consequently the inadequacy of the
term. In *The Lonely Londoners* (London, 1956) the city slickers
of Port-of-Spain find themselves in a real city at last, the very
centre of the Empire on which the sun seldom rises. It is in London
that they realise the smallness of Port-of-Spain. There is a passage
where there is a huge clock which can tell what time it is in every
capital city of the world. He looks for Trinidad to find out what
time it is in Port-of-Spain, and succeeds in finding it only with
with greatest difficulty.

The point is well made, since Galahad regards this date as the
first of his great achievements in conquering the big city. The
passage symbolises the central encounter in the book between the
parochial consciousness of the West Indians, and the vast chaos
of London. Galahad, no doubt, may seem as insignificant and
out of place in London as Port-of-Spain appears beside the great
cities of the world. Yet Trinidad time is going to be imposed on
the ponderous rhythms of Big Ben.

The 'boys', as Selvon calls his innocents abroad, reconstruct
the 'lime' and the language of the 'lime', and through imposing

their language on the great city, they remake it in their own image. Sometimes they shrink it by the use of a reductive simile. Hoary Paddington slums reveal walls which are cracking 'like the last days of Pompeii'. The winter sun, symbol of the devitalised misery of the megalopolis, is 'like a force-ripe orange'. The 'boys', who have originated from a world of language, recreate in the big city a world of words in which they move, and through which they grope for clarity in the midst of experience as bewildering and vague as the London fog.

Catapulted into a strange world, their experience is as strange as was Tiger's in *A Brighter Sun*. They face a similar process of having to make sense of a bewildering milieu; like Tiger, the Creoles begin to ask questions about existence itself, about identity and manhood. But the 'boys' remain fragmented, partial personalities. They continue to be identifiable in terms of idiosyncrasy; they have nicknames, not real names. Perhaps nicknames are an acknowledgement of individual richness of personality, but they are also suggestive of an incompleteness of self. This is definitely the case in Naipaul's *Miguel Street*, which seems to owe much to early Selvon. In *The Lonely Londoners*, it is the group that has a full self, that faces the wilderness and survives; not to belong is to be lost in the void.

The term 'the boys' begins to gain weight as the book proceeds. It indicates not only the strange pre-moral innocence which Selvon's people seem to preserve wherever they are, but a certain immaturity, which persists because these calypsonians refuse to awaken to responsibility, even under the weight of metropolitan pressures. Thus Selvon contrasts Galahad's 'grand-change' (bluff) with Moses' growing gloom; the seemingly eternal youth of the group, with Moses' sense of Time and inanition; their irresponsibility, with Moses' weight of life, the burden of consciousness which he has just barely begun to assume, as he absorbs each man's folly, failure and momentary triumph.

By the end of the book, Moses sounds more like Sergeant Pepper than the calypsonian Lord Kitchener. He is singing the genuine urban blues. He sees laughter as part of a tragic process. Like a Wilson Harris consciousness (it seems inadequate to speak of a Harris 'character'), he feels the weight of each man's experience:

> Sometimes listening to them, he look in each face, and he feel a great compassion for every one of them, as if he live each of their lives, one by one, and all the strain and stress come to rest on his own shoulders.

It is no accident that the boys gather at Moses' place 'every Sunday morning . . . like if it is confession'. Moses by the end of the book

has a high priest's role; he greets the new arrivals and tries, reluct-
antly, in contrast to his Biblical namesake, to guide them through
the wilderness. But near the end of the book, one sees him on the
banks of the Thames, contemplating the aimlessness of things.

Here, his function is similar to that of Lamming's Old Man in
In the Castle of My Skin, in that he becomes a repository for group
consciousness, a sort of archetypal old man, a Tiresias figure. Is
it accident, or design, that this technique of moving from a frag-
mentary form, where several voices share the stage, to a point
where all the voices are blended either in chorus as in Mais's
Brother Man, or into the single representative voice of an archetypal figure, has occurred in all of these early writers? And what
about the technique as it appears in Brathwaite's Trilogy? How
much is owed there to the structure of T. S. Eliot's 'Waste Land',
and how much to the instinctive groping for an architecture,
appropriate to expressing the crucial tensions in West Indian
societies between the group and the privacy of the individual
soul, which these early writers seem to have done?

NOTES

1 See Ramchand, K. *The West Indian Novel and its Background*. London, 1970,
  chapter VI.
2 See Crowley, D. J. 'The Midnight Robbers,' *Caribbean Quarterly*, IV (1956),
  pp. 263-74.
3 Gomes, A. *Trinidadian Guardian*, 12 February 1947.
4 Gomes, A. 'Through a Maze of Colour', Unpublished MS.
5 In Howes, B. (ed.). *From the Green Antilles*.

From 'The Folk in Caribbean Literature', *Tapia* (17 December
1972), pp. 7-8, 13-14 (13-14). (Revised version of a paper
presented at the ACLALS Conference held at Mona, Jamaica,
January 1971.)

SELECTED BIBLIOGRAPHY

PROSE FICTION

Anthony, Michael. *The Year in San Fernando*. London, 1965.
Anthony, Michael. *Green Days by the River*. London, 1967.
Barrett, Lindsay. *Song for Mumu*. London, 1967.
Clarke, Austin. *Amongst Thistles and Thorns*. London, 1965.
Harris, Wilson. *Palace of the Peacock*. London, 1961.
Harris, Wilson. *The Far Journey of Oudin*. London, 1961.
Harris, Wilson. *The Whole Armour*. London, 1962.
Harris, Wilson. *The Secret Ladder*. London, 1963.
Harris, Wilson. *Tumatumari*. London, 1968.
Hearne, John. *Voices Under the Window*. London, 1955.
Hearne, John. *The Land of the Living*. London, 1961.
James, C. L. R. *Minty Alley*. London, 1936.
Lamming, George. *In the Castle of My Skin*. London, 1953.
Lamming, George. *Of Age and Innocence*. London, 1958.
Lamming, George. *Natives of My Person*. London, 1972.
Lovelace, Earl. *The Schoolmaster*. London, 1968.
Marshall, Paule. *The Chosen Place, The Timeless People*. New York, 1969.
McKay, Claude. *Banana Bottom*. New York, London, 1933.
Mais, Roger. *The Three Novels of Roger Mais*. London, 1966. (Each novel first published separately: *The Hills Were Joyful Together*. London, 1953; *Brother Man*. London, 1954; *Black Lightning*. London, 1955.)
Mendes, Alfred. *Pitch Lake*. London, 1934.
Mittelholzer, Edgar. *Corentyne Thunder*. London, 1941.
Mittelholzer, Edgar. *A Morning at the Office*. London, 1950.
Mittelholzer, Edgar. *The Life and Death of Sylvia*. London, 1953.
Mittelholzer, Edgar. *My Bones and My Flute*. London, 1955.
Naipaul, V. S. *Miguel Street*. London, 1959.
Naipaul, V. S. *A House for Mr Biswas*. London, 1961.
Naipaul, V. S. *The Mimic Men*. London, 1967.
Naipaul, V. S. *In A Free State*. London, 1971.
Patterson, Orlando. *The Children of Sisyphus*. London, 1964.
Reid, V. S. *New Day*. New York, 1949.
Reid, V. S. *The Leopard*. London, 1958.
St Omer, Garth. *Shades of Grey*. London, 1968.
St Omer, Garth. *J—, Black Bam and the Masqueraders*. London, 1972.
Salkey, Andrew. *A Quality of Violence*. London, 1959.
Salkey, Andrew. (Ed.), *Stories from the Caribbean*. London, 1965.
Salkey, Andrew. (Ed.), *Caribbean Prose*. London, 1967.
Selvon, Samuel. *A Brighter Sun*. London, 1952.
Selvon, Samuel. *The Lonely Londoners*. London, 1956.
Selvon, Samuel. *Moses Ascending*. London, 1975.
Stewart, John. *Last Cool Days*. London, 1971.
Williams, Denis. *Other Leopards*. London, 1963.

POETRY

Bennett, Louise. *Jamaica Labrish*. Jamaica, 1966.
Brathwaite, Edward. *The Arrivants*. London, 1973. (First published in three vols: *Rights of Passage*. London, 1967; *Masks*. London, 1968; *Islands*. London, 1969.)
Brathwaite, Edward. *Other Exiles*. London, 1975.
Brown, Wayne. *On the Coast*. London, 1972.
Figueroa, John. (Ed.), *Caribbean Voices*. London, 1971. (First published in two vols: Vol. 1, London, 1966; Vol. 2, London, 1970.)
Hendriks, A. L. *Madonna of the Unknown Nation*. London, 1974.
McNeill, Anthony. *Reel from 'The Life Movie'*. Kingston, 1975. (This edition 'replaces' the 1st edition of 1972.)
Morris, Mervyn. *The Pond*. London, 1973.
Salkey, Andrew. (Ed.), *Breaklight*. London, 1971.
Scott, Dennis. *Uncle Time*. Pittsburgh, 1973.
Walcott, Derek. *The Castaway*. London, 1965.
Walcott, Derek. *The Gulf*. London, 1969.
Walcott, Derek. *Another Life*. New York, London, 1973.
Walcott, Derek. *Sea Grapes*. London, New York, 1976.

PLAYS

Gilkes, Michael. *Couvade*. London, 1974.
Hill, Errol. *Man Better Man*, in John Gassner (ed.), *The Yale School of Drama Presents*. New York, 1964.
John, Errol. *Moon on a Rainbow Shawl*. London, 1958.
Walcott, Derek. *Dream on Monkey Mountain and other plays*. New York, 1970; London, 1972.

CRITICAL STUDIES

Books
Gilkes, Michael. *Wilson Harris and the Caribbean Novel*. London, 1975.
Harris, Wilson. *Tradition, the Writer and Society*. London and Port-of-Spain, 1967.
James, Louis. (Ed.), *The Islands in Between*. London, 1968.
Maes-Jelinek, Hena. *The Naked Design: a reading of 'Palace of the Peacock'*. Aarhus, 1976.
Moore, Gerald. *The Chosen Tongue*. London, 1969.
Ramchand, Kenneth. *The West Indian Novel and its Background*. London, 1970.
Ramchand, Kenneth. *An Introduction to the Study of West Indian Literature*. London, 1976.
Walsh, William. *V. S. Naipaul*. London, 1973.
White, Landeg. *V. S. Naipaul: a critical introduction*. London, 1975.

Articles (in addition to those from which extracts have been given in this anthology)
Baugh, Edward. 'Metaphor and Plainness in the Poetry of Derek Walcott', *Literary Half-Yearly*. Vol. 11, July 1970, pp. 47-58.
Baugh, Edward. *West Indian Poetry 1900-1970* (pamphlet). Kingston, 1971.

Baugh, Edward. 'Questions and Imperatives for a Young Literature', *Humanities Association Review*. Vol. 24, Winter 1973, pp. 13-24.

Brathwaite, Edward. 'The African Presence in Caribbean Literature', *Daedalus*. Vol. 103, Spring 1974, pp. 73-109. (Reprinted in Sidney W. Mintz (ed.), *Slavery, Colonialism and Racism*. New York, 1974.)

Dathorne, O. R. 'Africa in the Literature of the West Indies', *Journal of Commonwealth Literature*. No. 1, September 1965, pp. 95-116.

Drayton, Arthur D. 'The European Factor in West Indian Literature', *Révue des Langues Vivantes*. Vol. 36, 1970, pp. 582-601.

Ismond, Patricia. 'Walcott versus Brathwaite', *Caribbean Quarterly*. Vol. 17, September-December 1971, pp. 54-71.